In a Summer Garment

In a Summer Garment

*The Experience
of an Autistic Child*

Ann Lovell

Secker & Warburg
London

First published in England 1978 by
Martin Secker & Warburg Limited
14 Carlisle Street, London W1V 6NN

Copyright © 1978 Ann Lovell

SBN: 436 26055 7

Parts of this book first appeared in the form of articles in
the *Guardian*, the *Daily Telegraph*, *Mother* and *Vogue*.

The poem "Fire and Ice" by Robert Frost from *The Poetry of
Robert Frost* edited by Edward Connery Lathem is reproduced by
permission of Jonathan Cape Limited, London, and Holt,
Rinehart & Winston, New York, and the Estate of Robert Frost.

Dr Lorna Wing's summary, "The Handicaps of Autistic Children",
first appeared in the 10th Anniversary edition of *Communication*,
the journal of the NSAC, and is reproduced by permission of Dr
Wing and *Communication*; the material from *Early Childhood
Autism* by Dr Lorna Wing is reproduced by permission of
the author and Pergamon Press Limited.

Filmset in Great Britain by
Northumberland Press Ltd, Gateshead, Tyne and Wear
Printed and bound by
Richard Clay (The Chaucer Press) Ltd,
Bungay, Suffolk

To my children

And yet are there other beggars, apparently in health,
But wanting in their wits, both men and women,
Those that are lunatic, lolling and leaping
Or sit about as mad as the moon, more or less.
They care not for the cold, nor take account of heat,
But move according to the moon; moneyless they wander,
With a good will, but witless, over many wide counties,
Just as Peter did, and Paul, save that they preach not
And do no miracles; but many times it happens
That they utter prophecy, all as if in play;
God suffers such to go, and it seems to my judgement
They are his apostles, such people, or his privy disciples;
For he sent them forth silverless, in a summer garment,
Barefoot and breadless, and they beg of none ...

... Men of this manner, Matthew teaches us
We should have into our houses and help them when they come
For they are merry mouthed men, minstrels of heaven,
God's boys, the Bible says, jesters of Jesus;
Under his secret seal their sins are covered ...

William Langland, *Vision of Piers Plowman*

Simple Simon met a pieman, going to the fair.
Said Simple Simon to the pieman,
Let me taste your ware.
Said the pieman to Simple Simon,
Show me first your penny.
Said Simple Simon to the pieman,
Indeed I have not any.

Nursery Rhyme

The author would like to thank the National Society for Autistic Children for their help and cooperation; also the British Society for Music Therapy and the Riding for the Disabled Association.

Contents

Preface

Early Childhood Autism

In 1943, a well known American psychiatrist, Leo Kanner, published an article in which he described a group of abnormal behaviour characteristics in children as having a common pattern, thus differentiating them from the general mass of abnormality. The group came to be known as "Kanner's Syndrome", although the name he gave to it was "early infantile autism".

In the book *Early Childhood Autism*, published in 1967, and edited by Dr Lorna Wing, of the Medical Research Council Social Psychiatry Unit, Institute of Psychiatry, London, Dr Wing lists the five abnormalities which Kanner regarded as being crucial to making a diagnosis.

(a) A profound lack of affective contact with other people.
(b) An anxiously obsessive desire for the presence of sameness.
(c) A fascination for objects which are handled with skill with fine motor movements.
(d) Mutism, a kind of language that does not seem to be intended to serve interpersonal communication.
(e) The retention of an intelligent and pensive physiognomy and good cognitive potential, manifested, in those who can speak, by feats of memory and, in the mute children, by their skill on performance tests, especially the Seguin form board.

Lorna Wing emphasizes that these five points are simply a brief abstraction from the complex clinical picture, and are open to misinterpretation. When making a diagnosis it is important to refer to Leo Kanner's detailed clinical descriptions which bring to life the strange behaviour of the classically autistic children whom he observed over many years.

She goes on to point out that Kanner gave his name to the typical or nuclear autistic syndrome. In research work it is essential to be precise in the use of diagnostic terms, in order to make possible comparisons between different studies. However, there are many children who have features of the autistic pattern, and who need the same kind of management and education, but who cannot be said to have Kanner's syndrome. There is no neat dividing line between typical autism and these other conditions. The autistic syndrome shades into the personality that is untalkative, unsociable and pedantic, but within the normal range, and, at the other extreme, into a severe form of mental retardation.

Lorna Wing also writes that it is most important to remember that the severity of the condition is not uniform in all children and this too makes diagnosis more difficult. She then goes on to give her own description of the elements making up the autistic behaviour pattern. This is based upon Kanner's paper, but, unlike Kanner, Lorna Wing organizes the items into a logical scheme, to make it easier to use in clinical practice or in research.

Such descriptions and classifications represent knowledge I neither had, nor dreamed of having, before Simon was born in 1962. Oddly enough, I had once heard of autism when, in 1956, a fellow student at Cambridge was telling me about a psychology lecture on the subject that he had just been attending. He had been fascinated by Kanner's theory concerning the cause of the condition (the cause, in fact, is still unknown): Kanner had observed that most of the parents of the children he had interviewed were highly educated, intelligent people, many from professional backgrounds, and that they were extremely reserved and cold in their manner. He therefore formed a theory of causation known as the "refrigerator parents" theory: early childhood autism was caused by a lack of parental affection and warmth.

I remember shivering slightly at the idea of such parents doing so much damage to their children. I was thinking of getting married myself, to someone who was highly intelligent and highly educated. Could we ever behave like that to our children? I could not conceive of treating a child without love. Quickly, I shrugged the idea aside. A passing shadow had brushed me. The little piece of information rolled away into depths of memory, and life went on, busy, crowded, exciting. Ten years later, I was to discover how the little conversation had been preserved.

For it was, indeed, a full ten years before I came across the word again. I had left university, held a job as an advertising copywriter for three years, married, and retired into childbearing without hearing it mentioned again. I had totally missed out on any publicity surrounding the condition, and certainly had never set eyes on an affected child.

This is not really surprising. The National Society for Autistic Children, the organization responsible in Britain for the setting up of most of the educational facilities and for all of the publicity given to the plight of autistic children, was founded only in 1962, by a group of parents desperate to secure help and teaching for their children. Until the work of the Society and the National Society for Autistic Children in the USA and their equivalents in other countries began to make some impact, the public at large, and, indeed, a wide section of the medical profession, was in complete ignorance of Kanner's syndrome.

Today, the picture has changed. Publicity in all the media, appeals, conferences, the success of special schools have all contributed to rouse interest in these extraordinary children and their difficulties. But the interest is still not great enough. It does not always lead to action. Autism is still not recognized by the Department of Education and Science in Britain as a separate handicap, worthy of its own special schools such as those for the deaf, the blind or the spastic – this, despite the acknowledged success of the special schools started by the Society. Far too many autistic children find their way into mental sub-normality hospitals, where they only deteriorate, and lead a life devoid of purpose or significance. I frequently find myself giving talks to large groups of parents who only have the haziest notion of what autism is and what it means in terms of everyday life. Once they understand, they are more than willing to help, either financially or practically. And the help, the understanding, is needed, urgently.

The beautiful, intelligent faces of autistic children lend themselves to romantic, wildly inaccurate pictures of them as displaced, misunderstood human beings, the "Midwich Cuckoos" of modern society. Living with a severely disturbed autistic child is not romantic – it is reality at its most harsh. The parents have to struggle to find their own path to accepting this reality. Some never make it, and give up. Some, I think most, only make it with help. A very few have been strengthened by previous training and life experience, and get there on their own.

Since the child's main hope of achieving some kind of happy and useful place in society is founded on this initial acceptance by the parents, it seems to me that it is of vital importance to help them reach it. The families of autistic children need support – all of them – both parents and siblings. Any one area will only contain a few autistic children, so that the families are particularly prone to feelings of isolation. They are, indeed, out on a very solitary limb. In Britain membership of the National Society for Autistic Children, or one of its area branches, certainly helps, but this tends to be in a general way, and not on a day-to-day basis. Most people are afraid of the responsibility of, say, babysitting for, or taking out an autistic child. Yet the parents, the brothers and sisters, have that responsibility every day of their lives. It imprisons them and marks their every decision, changing the whole tenor of their lives. They need help.

The words that Dilys sang at the concert at Somerset Court, the last few lines of the twenty-third psalm which close this book, are still very far from true for autistic children in general. Which is why I have written it.

1

The Son and Heir

My experience with Simon follows a pattern which I have found to be almost classical, which is why an accurate description of it may be helpful to many. It differs from the majority of cases I have known only in the lesser degree of severity of the handicap. With Simon, I have been allowed to escape the worst impact of autistic behaviour in that he has never been hyper-active, nor self-destructive. On the other hand it is possibly the absence of these two frequently found abnormalities which prevented our recognizing the nature of the problem earlier, so that I paid in a longer period of acute anxiety for what I gained in peaceful nights.

It is, to my mind, one of the most exquisitely cruel aspects of early childhood autism that it only becomes apparent to the parents very slowly that there is anything wrong with the child. If they are experienced in the care of small children, they may spot the clues more quickly than I did, but in the majority of cases, the autistic child is the first born, which means that the parents are new to the job, and have no yardstick by which to measure. Thus, though oddities of behaviour may be striking enough to produce flickers of doubt and uncertainty, the parents are liable to be too unsure of themselves to persist in the face of reassurances from grandparents, neighbours, friends, GPs or Doctor Spock – who, themselves, may very well never have encountered an autistic child. This was true in Simon's case (although I exempt Doctor Spock from criticism, since his book *Baby and Child Care*, the motherhood bible of my generation, is mainly concerned with normal babies).

1

I had been anxious throughout most of this, my first pregnancy. It was an intensely wanted one. The recent death of a friend's baby, at the age of three months, from sudden bronchitis, had made me almost morbidly aware of the infinite frailty of babies. I was afraid for mine. There seemed little cause. Apart from a drop in the haemoglobin level which necessitated iron injections, and a somewhat heavy fall on an icy path at seven months, which alarmed no one but myself, it was an entirely normal pregnancy. I remained very healthy. Attendance at childbirth training classes run by the National Childbirth Trust helped bring about a moderately easy, and quite normal first birth, without anaesthetics. Simon was born in hospital, with all due medical care. The only outstanding thing about our son and heir, when he finally emerged, was that he was nowhere near so ugly as I had been led to expect. This is not maternal bias, as my two subsequent babies were as blue, and wrinkled, and puffy as the textbook could wish. Simon, from the moment he was put into my arms after his birth, was pink, and smooth, and perfect, so perfect that all the anxieties of pregnancy fell away at once, and I smiled at my own stupidity. Of course he was beautiful. I was not physically deformed, and I was married to a healthy, good-looking man. I had every right to expect so marvellous a baby.

The nurses in the maternity ward shared my views. During my eight-day stay, they were constantly bearing Simon off to display to friends and visitors – often without bothering to tell me first. I glowed with pride. Even his cry was pure and truly pitched (again, no foolish bias – those of his sister and brother were like peacocks in the mating season).

Nobody, but nobody, suggested or to my knowledge thought that there was anything wrong with this beautiful baby, weighing over eight pounds, feeding hungrily and easily at the breast, behaving like every other baby in the ward. I was very happy and proud when at last I took him home to our new house.

There followed then a typically awful period of readjustment. Many mothers have known it. I had been used to an interesting job in a busy office, to meeting a constant variety of people, to constant stimulus. Now I found myself on my own with a new baby in a new place where I knew virtually nobody, and with no experience of full-time housekeeping and child care. The cooker in that house still sticks in my mind as the symbol of that period. It was an old Raeburn stove – the kind that is nowadays the symbol of good, country living, with a bubbling stock-pot and crusty home-made bread. Whilst my husband was still on "holiday" from the office, caring for me, I did not suspect its fiendish nature. Only after he had returned to work, leaving me to manage alone, did the full extent of its devilishness become revealed. I simply could not keep it alight. No book of words had survived to help me. I tried everything. If I ran it at an incessant high heat so that I could at least cook, I splintered the fire bricks. If I let it burn low, it used to wait, I swear, until it heard me coming, and then promptly went out. I was tired to my bones. I had never known such tiredness. In fact, I was wallowing in a bad fit of post-natal depression, without in the least knowing what was the matter with me. There was no one to help, no one to talk to. I liked my new doctor, but he seemed terribly busy, and as the baby grew plumper and lustier every day, whilst I was not actually ill, I did not dare to appeal to him. I found the isolation and the loneliness appalling. So desperate was I for company, that I invited strange women encountered in the shops home to tea, in the hopes of finding a friend. I felt I was going mad, losing all sense of identity. Week after week I attended the Infant Welfare Clinic, but it was much more for my own sake than for the baby's, much more in the hope of meeting someone with whom I had something in common, than in recording the baby's regularly increasing weight. The latter, however, turned out to be the only satisfaction of the visit. His good looks increased with every pound that went on. At least old ladies stopped to admire him in the street. The little chat with them was superficial, but it was better than nothing. My husband could not help me. He had to travel a long way to work, and did not return until late in the evening. His busy world of work, which once I had shared, now seemed light years away.

I am deliberately making some play upon these feelings of loneliness and isolation, which lasted for over a year. It is not entirely out of self-pity, but because I think that this period of intense solitude built up barriers of defensiveness around Simon, myself, and our way of life. Simon had become the mainspring of my existence, and Simon was perfect. My husband also was perfect, but there was so little time to talk to him, and, much worse, so little to talk to him about.

By the time Simon was nine months old, by now a large, heavy, lazy baby, I began to wonder, as again I think many mothers do, if the coming of a second child might not help the situation. I was vaguely aware that I was concentrating too much on Simon. With two babies to care for I would be too busy to feel so constantly sorry for myself. We would be more of a proper family. We talked it over. My husband was of the same opinion. Before long, a second pregnancy was under way. A miscarriage intervened, but a third pregnancy was soon established, and looked like being secure.

Oddly enough, a lot of the peculiarly female reasoning behind the start of the second pregnancy turned out to be more sensible in the event than it seems as I write it down. Having lost the role of the bright, rising young copywriter, I had failed to find anything to replace it. One child was not enough. If I was going to be a wife and mother, I wanted to do the job thoroughly. As the pregnancy advanced, I became in many ways a lot happier. I found a friend living in the same road as myself, with a baby girl the same age as Simon, and we often visited each other.

All the same, it was during this pregnancy that the first flickers of anxiety appeared about Simon. Not unnaturally, both I myself and others tended to put them down to my physical state. The judgment of pregnant women is never entirely to be trusted. So the anxieties were dismissed, as adequately as a lawn-mower kills the daisies on the lawn.

The source of these anxieties, ironically enough, sprang from my new friendship. Simon was so much *slower* than Alexandra, Jane's little girl – slower in every way. Almost every time I returned home after visiting them, I reached for my Doctor Spock, and re-read the lovely, reasurring bit about comparisons being invidious, since no two babies are the same. Certainly, I reflected, closing the book, Simon and Alexandra weren't. He was still barely able to sit by himself, whilst she was already pulling herself up to her feet, and crawling all over the house, to the despair of her mother. But it wasn't just the slowness that worried me. It was the apathy. He was too placid, much as my friend envied me this shining virtue in my child. He seemed to take no interest in the world about him. He only really responded to physical contact – to tickling, horseplay and romping with his father, to cuddling. Words seemed to float past him, making no impact. He did not look you in the eye. I used to laugh as he stared woodenly past the old ladies who still bent over him, and called him stand-offish. It did not occur to me in my inexperience that that was not a term that could be applied to babies. Babies can be frightened, angry, nervous, hungry, sleepy, sick – but stand-offishness has to be learned. Compared with quick, light, inquisitive Alexandra, Simon seemed to lack something vital. I began to long for a display of the curiosity and interest in life that led to Alexandra's escapades.

At the Infant Welfare Clinic, which I still attended regularly, all was reassurance. Yes, I was told, Simon was late in reaching his milestones of development, wasn't he, but still, he did seem to reach them in the end, and he was a splendid baby. He passed the routine test for deafness with flying colours, though it had not occurred to me to worry about that as he so plainly heard me when I sang to him, which was a lot of the time.

Once more, the lawn-mower decapitated the daisies. We went away for a seaside holiday when Simon was fifteen months old, to a hotel that lived up to its reputation for offering facilities for young children. I was nearing the end of the uncomfortable first stage of pregnancy, and was glad of the rest. I was also glad to see Simon with a crowd of playfellows around him. I was, without knowing it, searching for more reassurance than the Clinic could give me. The vague feeling that all was not quite as it should be persisted, despite the fact that while we were at the hotel he at last abandoned immobility, and began to propel himself around by a technique known in the family as bottom shuffling. He quickly grew adept at this, especially once we had returned home where there were parquet floors, and achieved a turn of speed that put the mere crawlers to shame. He never did crawl.

My unease stemmed mainly from the fact that while other toddlers made advances, friendly or otherwise, to him, he never made any towards them. He did not seem in the least interested by their presence, but maintained a display of indifference that would have done credit to a Chinese diplomat. I still have a snapshot showing the puzzled face of a precocious little red head, obviously very taken by him, as Simon stared out to sea, over her shoulder. Gradually, the others learned to leave him alone. I was not too worried – I had read that young children of this age tend to play beside rather than with each other – but I would have expected Simon to show at least some awareness of his new companions.

Apart from this somewhat odd behaviour, he did not seem so very different from the other babies. He ate and slept well, and made no more fuss than the rest of them over the strangeness of the place. He was saying a few words, mostly nouns, by now, and in this respect there were certainly others like him. He was still, relatively speaking, a peaceable, easy-going baby.

Soon after our return home, however, his character began to change. He discovered the sound of his own voice, and the potential volume of his own voice, and the value of it as a weapon. We had reached, and he wasn't in any way late about this, the tantrum stage.

Of course I had read about tantrums, and had, I thought, drilled myself into the art of dealing with them. I would be the perfect pupil of the Spock school, calm, firm, comforting in my unflappability. But I was ill-prepared for what was to come. The tantrums described in the books surely did not go on as long as these, nor were they so frequent, nor brought on by such an extraordinary array of causes. I had understood that tantrums were the young child's first attempt to express his own will as distinct from his mother's, his first experiment at being a person, as it were, in his own right. The tantrum, therefore, was usually caused by thwarting that new, personal will. Simon's screams, on the other hand, seemed to be provoked by anything and everything. True, he broke me in gently – it did not all happen at once – but I was a little taken aback by the situations that first began to provoke them. He suddenly began to dislike going to tea with my one and only friend, and would begin to scream the moment we arrived and began to chat, to the point where we could no longer hear each other. He hated going into shops – and it was not long before I began to dread going into shops too. He was terror-stricken by dogs, and no amount of patient chat with old, resigned Labradors would abate his fear – or his screams. He could bear nothing shiny near his face – one visit to the hairdresser's was enough to convince me, and the hairdresser, that

Simon's hair-do would have to be strictly do-it-yourself. As he grew older, so the list of tantrum-causers grew, reaching its maximum by the time he was about five.

At eighteen months, however, it still seemed to me that I simply had a child with an excessively strong will. This characteristic runs on both sides of the family, so it did not dismay me, or my husband, unduly. Besides, I had found a powerful ally, not mentioned in the books, in the form of music. I had, as I have said, always sung to Simon, and encouraged him to sing with me. He had a marvellous ear for music, and sang beautifully in tune. I discovered that, even if a tantrum was in full throat, I could calm it right down by putting on a record, preferably a classical one. The structured, harmonious music of the eighteenth century evoked the quickest response, and the howling monster would be transformed to an entranced statue. I knew of no other child upon whom music had so marked an effect. Perhaps Mozart or Bach or Beethoven had been like this as children, perhaps this explained the oddness, the inaccessibility – our perfect baby was perhaps a musical genius. The intelligence, the sensitivity of his features seemed to lend feasibility to this theory (which of course I did not have the nerve to mention to anyone). Slow he might be, but the slowness did not seem to be that of poor intellect, rather the result of great reflection.

That Autumn, when I was some two-thirds of the way through the pregnancy, my brother and sister-in-law from Brazil came to visit us. There was some excitement about this on my part, as they had not seen Simon before, but the excitement did not affect him. He received their attentions with the same unconcern that he displayed towards anyone outside the immediate family. Childless themselves, they did not appear to notice anything unusual about his behaviour. They, no more than we, had no yardstick by which to measure.

Soon after this visit, I started going to ante-natal training classes again. This marked the end of that first period of loneliness and isolation, for at the training class I made several friends, and the decision to start a local branch for the National Childbirth Trust gave me the much needed outlet for all the accumulated mental energy. There was absolutely no more time to feel sorry for myself. I had my own baby to work for and look forward to, and also those of my friends and their friends, for the Branch simply mushroomed from the evening of its inauguration in a way which spoke eloquently for the social need it was answering. In my case, I think it saved my sanity.

Joanna was born at home. I have an inborn dislike of institution life, and did not relish the prospect of another stay in hospital, especially as this would have meant leaving Simon. We had an excellent midwifery service in our district, the last birth had been normal, the doctor was willing – there seemed to be no sound objection. Our respective families could not help us out, so we solved the problem of caring for Simon by engaging a temporary Nannie-cum-Mother's Help. Jeannette was young, but she was a trained Nursery Nurse, and, when she discovered that we intended to treat her as a younger sister rather than as a hireling, she threw herself into the task of jollying Simon into responding to her with a devotion that I found very moving to see. She succeeded, too. At twenty-one months, he was still not walking, though he could pull himself upright. Even the books agreed that this was a little late, though "still within the range of the normal". (It is only now, in middle life, that I see the almost total meaninglessness of that phrase!) Jeannette was determined that he should be walking before she left at the end of her eight week stay, and I don't know which of us was the more pleased that she accomplished her objective. I have often noticed since how helping Simon seems to bring out the best in people.

The birth itself was a perfect advertisement for the training methods I had been taught. I spent the day up and about the house, the evening, after Simon had been put to bed, sitting in the rocking chair, and finally retired to bed half an hour before our daughter was born into the hands of our slightly breathless GP – the labour had been so painless that we had not realized how advanced it was, and had barely called him in time. It is quite rare, I believe, to have all the physical factors of the birth fitting together quite so harmoniously, and it was a marvellous experience. After it, I was neither tired nor depressed, which, in the light of events to come, was just as well. The only aspect of it that startled me was the extreme ugliness of the baby that emerged. I had expected another Simon, and actually voiced my disappointment, drawing a reproof from the midwife. In fact, by the end of the week, Joanna had sufficiently recovered from the speed of her entry into the world to show us that she was a pretty little girl, very delicate and feminine of feature, except when she was feeding, whereupon her eyes fixed into a concentrated glare of voracity. I had never seen that look of concentration in her brother's eyes at all, and I was struck by it.

His reaction to the birth was the one unhappiness amid so much joy. Even so, all my feelings were in such a state of upheaval that I did not have the lucidity to give a definite form to the shadow that fell over me then. I had expected Simon to be jealous, and clinging. How, I wondered, would he react to being left downstairs, in Jeannette's sole charge, while I lay upstairs in bed, devoting myself to his new sister? We had talked the matter through, of course, and his father had sought to pave the way to future good relations by buying him a large blue toy engine, which was placed cunningly in the crib for the moment of introduction. Nothing, however, went according to plan.

As soon as he awoke next morning, Jeannette and my husband brought him in to the room and took him to look into the wicker cradle where Joanna lay asleep. We watched him, smiling – what would he make of her? Then we realized that it was the engine he was looking at, not the baby. His father gave it to him, and told him it was a present from the baby, inviting him to look at her. Instead, clutching his loot to him, he headed for the door, without further attention to the rest of the contents of the cradle, and without so much as a glance at me. We were both crestfallen. We had not expected this. We explained it away by interpreting it as a somewhat unusual manifestation of jealousy. There *had* to be jealousy. All children experienced it upon the birth of a sibling. Of course it was jealousy.

But during the whole of the week I spent in and around bed, Simon hardly came near me. I could hear the record player going full blast downstairs with Jeannette's favourite *Red Army Ensemble*, belting out rousing Russian dance tunes. They seemed to be having a whale of a time. It was *I* who was jealous, *I* who felt rejected. He seemed to have transferred all his affection to someone else with incredible casualness. I could not understand it. Had I done something wrong? Did he really not love me at all? I would have preferred him to be clinging and whining, and aggressive towards Joanna – it would have been wearing, but it would have been, in my eyes, preferable to this hurtful indifference.

A couple of weeks after the birth, the Health Visitor came to pay her routine post-natal visit. She was new to the district, and I had not met her before. She asked the usual questions about the birth and the baby's progress. I did not notice how keenly she was observing Simon, as he played around the room, nor did I think there was anything unusual in her request that I should take him with me when I made my first visit to the Infant Welfare Clinic with Joanna. I had not the slightest idea that the first professional doubt as to Simon's well-being had just reared its head. I knew nothing of the report that went back to the Clinic doctor. The Health Visitor was not quite satisfied, and she wanted a medical opinion concerning the child. She followed routine procedure.

In the intervening years that procedure has been reviewed, and I think rightly. For if that report had gone to my family doctor, whom by now I had come to trust and respect after all the care I had received from him during miscarriage, pregnancy and birth, I might have been spared two whole years of agonizing worry. He knew me well enough to be direct with me. The Clinic doctor did not know me at all. We could not communicate, and, probably through no fault of her own, she always put me on the defensive.

The interview with her remains vivid in my memory. My hackles rose almost with the first question. Everything she said seemed to imply that I mismanaged my children. No doubt she meant to imply nothing of the sort, but by now I was growing sensitive on the subject of my strange son. She said nothing more direct in that interview than that he seemed to be playing round the perimeter of the room in a rather disturbed way, and I, furious by now, retorted that it was probably because he did not like the room very much. And that was that. I sat there loathing her, and cried with rage all the way home, vowing that I would never set foot in the place again. I never did, to my loss.

I regard that piece of non-communication as tragic. If only that doctor had explained her fears – and the reasons for her fears – tremendous pressures would have been lifted from Simon, from myself, and from my marriage. I would have been shocked, grieved, numbed – but I would have started then and there to look for the help we so sorely needed. Only a few months ago, I learned from a Health Visitor friend that at that time, fourteen years ago, it was not official policy to tell the mother when there was a fear of mental handicap. It was felt to be better for her to discover it for herself in the fullness of time. I often wonder now which committee members bear the responsibility for the formulation of that dreadful policy, which ignored so sovereignly the individuality of human beings. Certainly, they did me a great wrong.

Joanna continued to progress happily without the aid of the Clinic. I had enough new friends with children the same age to feel plenty of support around me. She developed at a pace far faster than her brother's had been at the same age, but then, girls, I told myself firmly, do develop faster as a rule.

All the same, I was by now worrying consciously about Simon. We had, after all, come under attack. His second birthday came and went. He walked confidently by now, if slowly, but he was not talking very much more than he had when we were on holiday the previous year. On the other hand, he could sing, and quite beautifully, with a repertoire ranging from operatic arias to little French folk songs. We could not converse together, so we sang. It wasn't very satisfactory for me, but it was better than nothing, and it did seem to give more substance to my private theory that I had a musical genius on my hands.

He continued to ignore his baby sister, and never displayed the least aggression towards her. Only when she was old enough to take a hand in it did their relationship develop. He played by himself, wherever he went.

His play, I noticed, puzzled, was not like other children's. It contained no imaginative quality whatsoever. He never, for instance, built up his collection of model cars into a car park, or brought them to some shoe-box garage – he used them for throwing across the room, or else, quite simply, for holding. The pleasure he obtained from a friction toy was not from the motion, even when he had been shown the technique many times, but from the buzzing sound. He would listen to this by the hour, a rapt expression on his face. The building bricks he used for skimming across the floor, so that they hit the skirting board with a gratifying crack – he never built anything with them unless an adult took charge. Painting or drawing meant nothing to him – even finger paints gave no pleasure, except to his incessantly inquisitive tongue. He tasted everything, and, what was worse, *liked* everything from scouring powder to salt. I think his stomach lining by now must be encrusted with salt, yet it has never made him sick. All toxic substances had to be excluded rigidly from household use – with Simon around, I felt that germs were less of a risk than poisoning. He liked the taste of human skin, and was forever mortifying me by sniffing and licking our visitors rather than greeting them.

This odd form of play did not develop in the next twelve months, though changes took place in the rest of his behaviour, and not always for the better. Far from becoming more sociable, he became less so. He switched from screaming whenever we went into a strange place to making a bee-line for the nearest cupboard door, and settling down to a session of opening and shutting it, quite gently, but with evident gratification. This was less hard on the ears, it is true, but I found it wearing on the nerves, as the cupboard in question nearly always seemed to contain the best glass. If I tried to remove him, the resulting tantrum brought the visit to a precipitate end anyway, so we always left him to it. He never broke anything, and he kept perfectly quiet. He did the same thing in shops, which was more difficult to contend with, as strangers always tried to drag him away, afraid for his fingers. He never did trap them. Obviously, it was hard to keep my mind on what I was about, and I made some odd purchases in those days. Yet once having found his door, he stuck to it. He never wandered off, nor attempted to come and find me.

Despite these substitutes for screaming in some situations, it had redoubled in others. He seemed to enjoy screaming. If he wanted something, he screamed, or else, more profitably, took me by the hand and led me to it. If he was given the wrong plate at mealtimes, he screamed. If any room or place was at all echoey, he screamed at the top of his lungs – and that, I swear, was for enjoyment at the reverberation of the sound. As time went by, the list of scream-provokers grew.

How, you may wonder, could I possibly not have realized that something was seriously wrong, how could I have been so blind?

The answer to that is two-fold. Firstly, I *did* know, sub-consciously, that something was wrong. I can remember looking at Simon's beautiful eyes, and feeling that there was something odd, something not quite right about them; was it the shape, or the look ...? But consciously I fought that knowledge with every weapon I could lay hands on, and I did not overlook one!

Secondly, few can appreciate the amount of reassurance I was subjected to, from all sides, all of it kindly, well meant, and all of it so terribly, terribly hurtful because, deep inside, I did not believe it. I was just unlucky, they said, and was up against an unusually difficult character. Ancestors were hauled up out of obscure depths of memory and called upon to explain their descendant's eccentricities. So he wasn't speaking properly yet? Well, a lot of children did not speak properly till much later than that – Winston Churchill, they say, did not speak till he was five. Look at him, he was a fine, healthy boy, he was just going through a phase – his mind had not caught up with his body, that was all. He would grow out of it. How many times did I hear that phrase? How many times more did I *want* to hear it – it could not be said often enough. It was my life-belt. I laughed, with the others, at my own absurd anxieties, still trying to cure the problem of the daisies with a lawn-mower.

My anxieties, however, were by now firmly, and widely rooted. They simply took refuge underground, and began to choke everything else. I stopped admitting to worry, but started apologizing for my son.

A change of house brought about a temporary improvement. The new place had a large garden, with trees that could absorb the volume of the screams. It was easier to run, and not too far from a good nursery school. On the other hand, it was a long way from the shops, and miles from any kind of community centre. We had no car – but then, I did not know what lay ahead. At the time, the move seemed a good idea.

That Autumn, when Simon was two and a half, he had a bowel infection which would not clear up with routine treatment from our doctor. We were sent to the paediatrician at the local hospital. He issued a stronger anti-biotic and sent a report to my doctor. It was all straightforward enough. But there was a post-script, scribbled in pencil, "I am not satisfied with this child's general development."

Those were the words that finally turned us into the path that led to enlightenment, though not, unfortunately, at once. My doctor decided to send us off to obtain a general assessment from the paediatrician at a well-known London teaching hospital. I went with relief. Someone, at last, seemed to feel as I did. I even went to the length of making a private appointment. This was too important for general clinics, and long queues ...

But everything went wrong. We duly turned up for our appointment at the paediatrician's office, not knowing that someone, somewhere, had bungled his appointments for the day. An hour and a half later, having allowed for all the visions of emergencies that had charitably filled my mind, I picked up his phone, and with some temper asked to know where he was. Contrition. Apologies. Did we still want to see him? Through gritted teeth I said we did indeed. We had to take a taxi to get to his clinic, a mile away. As the clinic was still in progress, we naturally had to wait. The grand total was now two hours. Simon clamped himself to a large rocking horse, with a look on his face that boded no good for the person unwise enough to try and prise him off. It took two of us to carry him into the interview, screaming blue murder. I felt like making it a chorus. A band of students, flanking their chief, looked upon us with interest.

Everyone, myself included, admired as he put a dexterous end to the screams by popping a tongue depressor into Simon's mouth, and one into each fist. The silence was awe-inspiring. It transformed my mood. I had a strong desire to giggle.

The subsequent interview lasted just over twenty minutes. I was asked a few questions, which I found hard to answer, and so was Simon, who fared even worse. He was also asked to do some drawings, and gamely responded with a few aimless scrawls plus a hole in the paper. And that was all. I could not voice all the long-concealed worries, tell him of all the myriad, tiny details that perplexed me. The long wait, the sleight of hand with the tantrum had somehow closed the doors to the possibility of any real communication. Yet I still believed him when he told me not to worry, that the child was late, but normal. So much depended on my believing him. I had already heard the same words many times, but not from an authority such as this. Surely I could believe him, trust him? Someone in his position must be able to judge better than I, even though I knew I had hardly told him anything. Determinedly, I took Simon home. Now we had something to hold on to.

A few days later, I met my own doctor in the street. He stopped to tell me that he had received the full report from the paediatrician, and that he was quite satisfied with the child's development. I remember his smile of pleasure as he told me – I think he was as pleased as I was. Now we could all settle down to enjoying Simon.

His third birthday passed. Joanna, herself now a toddler, as restless and inquisitive as her brother had been placid and apathetic, began to take him in hand. She literally forced him into a relationship he otherwise would never have experienced. I rejoiced to see him respond. She was a natural boss, and he a natural follower. She commanded, and he obeyed. She led him into mischief he would never have dreamed of on his own, using his superior height and strength to supplement her own. High shelves could no longer keep things safe from her, for Simon would simply be requested to fetch them down for her, and Simon always obeyed – happy to be of service. Heavy up-and-over garage doors no longer confined her to the garden, for Simon was strong enough to lift them sufficiently high for her to wriggle underneath, and then run off, callously abandoning him in her quest for adventure ... No one's life was dull with Joanna around. Before long it was plain to see that Simon was her adoring slave.

Summer came. Still he was not talking. Those few nouns that he had acquired when he was fifteen months were all that he possessed by way of speech. He never managed a sentence. On the other hand, we discovered that he could recite long poems – the ones that I often read to him of an evening – entirely by heart. This was something. If he could do this, speech must surely be just around the corner. It must be – he was now three and a half. We encouraged the recitations, praised him, tried to teach him more. But as we listened to him, we became uneasily aware that though he could repeat the words accurately enough, he had absolutely no clue as to their meaning. They did not *tell* him anything, give him any picture, they were just a string of sounds. I found that he could recite French just as well as English. The language did not matter, for it signified nothing.

To add to this perplexity, he was reacting ever more violently to an increasing range of sounds: cold water gushing into the washing machine was one of the worst – he would put his hands over his ears, turn red with distress, and eventually rush away up to his room to scream. The vacuum cleaner produced a similar effect, and so – this was harder to live with – did the continuous hum of adult voices in conversation. He hated crowds of people, and if he was invited to a party, would spend the entire time at a cupboard door – this would be so even at houses with which he was entirely familiar. The same thing happened at play-group, unless I happened to be playing the piano, whereupon he would come and sit upon my knee, which made Joanna jealous.

I could no longer reconcile the London paediatrician's words with Simon's behaviour. I did not want to return to pester our overworked doctor. I was deeply miserable. I tried to talk it through with my husband, only to find that he was as puzzled and miserable as I was. I begged my friends for their opinions, and received no comfort. They did not want to hurt me, and, in any case, they were not sure how I would have received their real feelings. Reticence prevailed. I developed chronic indigestion. In the end, it was fear of an ulcer or worse that drove me back to the surgery. I was sent off for X-Rays, which revealed nothing. Then, at last, my doctor twigged. Writing out yet another prescription for comfort of the stomach, "Are you still worrying about Simon?" he asked me.

Three-quarters of an hour later, I emerged from his surgery to face the glares of an overcrowded waiting room, geared to five minute appointments. We had finally decided to return to the local paediatrician, whose post-script had first started the action. He must have had his reasons for writing it. It was time now to find out what they were.

The interview took place in our local hospital. No students were present. A psychiatrist shared a desk with the paediatrician. The atmosphere was personal, but businesslike. We had only been kept waiting some ten minutes, and it was a National Health Service appointment.

I started the ball rolling by dissolving usefully into tears. "Useful" is in fact the correct word, because the tears took with them every remaining barrier. No one showed any impatience. As soon as I could, I poured out the details, withholding nothing. I answered their questions as accurately as possible, for I wanted them to know every last thing that had been worrying me. We were there for well over an hour.

When I had finished, the paediatrician vouchsafed no opinion, but asked me if I would bring Simon into the hospital for a few days, for tests and observation. I wonder if he realized the extent of the relief with which I agreed. At long last, someone was taking me at my word, someone was sharing the load, and was prepared to act. For the first time in years, I could feel like a sane human individual – the label "overanxious mother" had just been ripped off.

The hospital is one of the pioneers of the mother care for children in hospital movement, and this meant that to my joy I was allowed to come in with Simon and stay with him throughout. I could hardly have borne a separation from him at this crucial time, and still feel the gratitude I felt then for the humanity with which I was treated.

Any mother who has ever stayed in hospital with a sick child knows the length of the hospital day. It has a peculiar propensity to unroll itself endlessly, with meals as longed-for milestones, and the actual medical tests as apprehensively expected, ever-receding hurdles, standing in the path of the return to normal living. If your child is physically sick, there is, in all probability, quite a lot for you to do as you share in the less expert part of the nursing and general care. Simon, however, was not in the least physically ill, and my job was simply one of keeping him happy, amused, and, if possible, out of trouble. At least, that is how I saw it, then, forgetful of all that the word "observation" entailed. I was chiefly afraid that one of his famous tantrums might upset another child who really was ill. I shall never forget the corridor leading into the general part of the ward. Unfortunately for my peace of mind, it echoed, as Simon was quick to find out. I think he must have spent some fifty per cent of his time in hospital galloping up and down that corridor, whooping it up, with me in his wake, trying vainly to distract him. Nor do I forget the kindness of the sister smilingly telling me not to worry. They were all kind ...

The tests themselves were routine enough. A skull X-Ray

was taken, urine samples were checked, and, the only difficult one, a blood sample was required. By the time the doctor had secured the amount he needed, everyone else present was bleeding too.

The stay in hospital was short, however long it felt. I did not know it, but it was the end of a whole phase of my life. On the evening of the second day, the paediatrician came to see me. He asked me if I actually had any idea what was wrong with my son. I replied that my father-in-law and one of my friends had both suggested that he might be mildly autistic, though I myself had no real idea what the word meant. He nodded. "I am afraid they are right," he told me, very gently. "Simon is autistic. I am afraid that you have a long, hard road ahead of you."

He went on to tell me how best we could help ourselves, and Simon, suggesting books that we might read about the condition, and recommending that we join the recently formed National Society for Autistic Children. I shall never forget his directness, and his compassion. Later, I learned that he had a handicapped child of his own.

He made a further appointment to see me, this time along with my husband, and asked me to bring Joanna, as well as Simon. Then he said we could go home, and left me alone with Simon.

I looked at him. Nothing seemed real any more. He was certainly not real. It was as if he had just fallen to pieces in front of my eyes. Somehow, I had to find the strength to tell my husband when he came later on. Something gave it to me, because I can remember doing it with a calm quite exterior to myself. I did not feel calm. I did not feel anything at all. Everything – my way of life, my pride, my confidence, my whole outlook – had just been totally and irrevocably shattered. The numbness was merciful. It was better that I should realize slowly how much we, but above all, Simon, had lost.

2

Disinheritance

In 1966, at the time of Simon's diagnosis, I did not know that autistic meant mentally handicapped. From the little I had heard of Kanner's syndrome, years previously, I had thought that the term described a purely emotional disorder, induced by deprivation of parental affection. This did not seem to make sense, for whatever other faults I may have had as a mother, failure to give affection was not one of them – of that, at least, I was quite certain. It also implied that once the deprivation was put to rights, the condition would improve, probably to the point of being cured. My self-confidence was not strong enough to resist such implications. I set to work to make myself as unhappy as possible by thinking up everything I could possibly have done wrong. Had I talked enough to Simon when he was a baby? Should I have gone to him more quickly when he cried? Had I been patient enough? Over and over, round and round, down and down my mind whipped itself.

Fortunately, the arrival of the booklet *Autistic Children*, by Dr Lorna Wing, published by the National Association for Mental Health – part of the reading recommended by the paediatrician – put a stop to this unhealthy state of affairs. I read it avidly.

The contents came as both a shock and a relief. The shock was the realization that our son was actually handicapped, rather than disturbed, and that, as yet, no one had succeeded in finding the cause of the handicap. This meant, in turn, that no one, therefore, knew of a cure. I did not digest that immediately. I could not. The relief came as I went on to read the description of the symptoms, and I saw that all, but all,

19

of Simon's oddities of behaviour fitted into a general pattern. There actually were other children like him – like him, and much, much worse. I almost laughed aloud when I read of the so-called "islets of normality" which had misled so many other parents, as well as ourselves. Other children, it seemed, displayed fantastic feats of memory, extreme musical ability, and even near mathematical genius. Others also objected violently to dogs, or washing machines. We were not alone. I still find it an incomprehensible characteristic of human beings that we derive comfort from the discovery that others share our personal misfortunes. We cannot really bear to be alone. The comfort is real, and is probably the basis of all the self-help organizations. We ourselves joined the National Society for Autistic Children, though I at least could not immediately face with pleasure the thought of going up to London to meetings.

The facts brought relief, as I have said. They were, as far as they went, facts, and as such were better than formless, nightmare worries. But they could not stop for long the dizzying downward spiral into which I then plunged. Nothing could – or should. I had to mourn, for my loss was as great as any bereavement.

There was for me an exquisite irony in the discovery that my beautiful son was mentally handicapped. The blow was extraordinarily shrewd, as if delivered by a Karate expert. After it, nothing could ever be as it had been.

I am a graduate. I had spent seven years at university, both in France and England, studying first for a BA then for a doctorate before I finally left, without the latter, disillusioned with academic life, to take a job in advertising. By the end of this lengthy education, intelligence had risen to the top of the list of all virtues, human and divine. It had supplanted God. Not that I was intolerant towards those who were not endowed with it – quite the contrary – I regarded such intolerance as a kind of stupidity, the kind that sparks off wars. I was ready to like everyone who would let me. This included abnormal people. When, as a new mother, I first began to attend the Infant Welfare Clinic, I was careful to smile at the Mongol baby in its pram. I even went out of my way to make somewhat stilted conversation with its mother. I found this rather difficult, but never bothered to ask myself why. In fact, I was embarrassed. I did not know *how* to talk to or of this strange baby. Of course, it did not occur to me to invite the pair of them home to tea, despite my own loneliness. That would have meant becoming involved in their difficulties. I did not want to become involved – I could not, in other words, act positively towards them. I did not know it, but I was baulking at the reality of a relationship with them. I was frightened of it. Hiding the fear made me feel guilty, and ill at ease.

I actually came to recognize this fear for what it was, and the reason for it, one weekend when Joanna was about five months old. I found her, one warm afternoon, covered with a highly suspect rash. It so happened that my period was more than three weeks overdue, and that I had never had German measles. The doctor, when he came, was not prepared to swear that the rash was innocuous. We both knew that if it *was* German measles, this was the worst possible time for me to catch it from the point of view of damage to a possible foetus. Panic. Gamma globulin. All of a sudden, the world of the mentally handicapped had touched mine. No! I could not face the possibilities. In my distress, I rang up a close friend, older than myself, and poured out my anxieties. I was frantic. I can clearly remember telling her that although I knew I could love and cherish a physically handicapped child, and help it, and teach it, I could never live with a mentally handicapped one. If I caught German measles, I told her, I was going to abort that baby.

So much for my tolerance. So much for my quasi-mystic belief in the powers of the human mind, which excluded neatly from consideration a significant minority of the human race. The Christian beliefs of my childhood and adolescence, discarded at university, pending inquiry, as it were, had been replaced by a very ill-planned structure, which did not stand up to any kind of real examination. A human being with an impaired mind was not to me a complete human being. He or she was not, therefore, to me, a lovable human being. I could never, under any circumstances, love such a person. I had distinctly spoken those very words to my friend, that frightened day. And it never dawned on me that I was being anything but the liberal, tolerant adult I believed myself to be – that I was, in fact, more prejudiced than most.

In the event, Joanna's rash was not, after all, German

measles. Nor was I pregnant – the late period appeared with gratifying promptness two days after I had had the injection of gamma globulin. The catastrophe was, it seemed, averted. I could safely return to my worship of perfect humanity incarnated in my two beautiful children – for a little while longer.

Now, two years later, I had just discovered that I was after all, and had been all the time, the mother of a handicapped child, of someone who – to quote my own words – "was not a complete human being", "someone I could never love".

And that was the catch, the great, vital flaw in all my previous thinking, and at the same time the thread that was eventually to lead me out of this terrifying labyrinth into which I had fallen: I *did* love him. I had loved him from the moment he was born – from before that, even. This was a love far too strong, far too primitive, to be denied now. I could not, after all, possibly be afraid of Simon. He was no frightening stranger. He was, and would always be, my own dear son. He needed all my love, and all my help, more than ever, because he was not what I had thought him to be – perfect.

This realization was fundamental. It was the rock on which we could build. Its discovery made every moment of distress and grief into something positive, even though I did not always know it at the time, and, indeed, did not really come to know it for many years. Simon's diagnosis changed the course of our lives, at once, and for ever, but the change it brought to the quality of our lives only came about slowly.

Two big readjustments, nonetheless, had to be made at once, grief or no grief. One was the attitude to the rest of the world that I adopted as we went about our daily lives; the other was my everyday handling of Simon himself.

The first was the harder, because, obscurely, I felt it had to be assumed at once, before I had had time to come to terms with my feelings. I had to learn how to meet pity which hurt my pride, sympathy which encouraged my own self-pity, and, worst of all, disbelief – the "you don't want to go trusting psychiatrists" school. Friends without number told me that "Simon will grow out of it, you'll see". They did not mean to make things harder for me, but they succeeded in doing so. The fact was, that Simon did not *look* mentally handicapped. Just as this had caused my own sore perplexity, so it was to continue to perplex other people. The following incident is a graphic example of this:

We were waiting for an appointment, some little time after the diagnosis, at our local dental hospital. Simon's introduction to dental treatment had to be very slow and gradual, in view of his fear of shiny objects near his head, and the consultant, after a letter from me, had pronounced himself interested and eager to help in any way. We sat, Simon and I, in a row of chairs near a pair of swing doors. A disabled patient approached on crutches and paused in front of the doors, smiling at Simon, clearly expecting him to jump up and hold them open for him. I did not register the situation for several seconds, and sat without reacting. The patient then asked Simon to hold the doors for him. There was, of course, no reaction. Simon merely stared past the man's ear in his usual stand-offish manner. The smile faded, and the man repeated his request loudly, with precisely the same result. At that moment I came too, and leapt to my feet to hold the door, with a hasty explanation to stem the flood of invective that was about to break out. The man stared at me, stared disbelievingly at Simon, and went his way. I sat down, rather shaken.

I had said that he was mentally handicapped, rather than "autistic". I quickly found that people in general did not understand me if I used the accurate term. They were ready enough to be compassionate if I said mentally handicapped, but autism meant little or nothing: it was one of those weird words psychiatrists love, and was therefore suspect. The situation is not so greatly changed today, ten years later. Perhaps more people have heard of the word, but I am still constantly being asked what it means, what is actually wrong with the child.

I myself used the words mentally handicapped if I was appealing for tolerance towards the child, without fully understanding the implications even of so general a term when it came to the position of that child in society. Perhaps my hardest collision with reality ever was the realization that my son was now entirely dispossessed. He would never vote. He could never own any property. He was not, in the eyes of the law, an independent person. Nor could he move freely about the world even with his family. Should we have wished to emigrate, certain countries would not have welcomed us with Simon. He was, and would be for all his life, dependent on the goodwill of others. I had not been alone in my previous views that mentally handicapped people were not complete human beings. What then were they? What sort of life could they have?

Because I loved Simon, I sprang immediately to his and their defence – again, long before I was ready, rationally or emotionally. I became aggressive, and probably over-protective, but at least I began to take my first steps in the right direction, the positive one.

No steps, however, were made without pain. Amongst my friends of all categories I could not help but be aware of a certain change of status. I was no longer like all the rest. They had to be careful how they spoke to me, and choose their words cautiously. I had stepped into the shoes of the mother of the Mongol baby. No one knew quite how to talk to me any more. Just as I had been, now they, too, were frightened. And that fear hurt me bitterly. I needed to talk. I blamed them for it, forgetting my own past history. My only weapon to counter it was to demonstrate, as hard as I could, my own complete acceptance of the situation, to show them that if I could relax about it, then so too could they, and accept Simon as I did. How I worked at it . . . and how frustrated I became.

This is the point, I think now, when we all really needed a good deal of professional help. We did not get it, I think largely owing to the success of my own determined efforts to show that we did not need it. The local psychiatric welfare worker visited us occasionally, as did the Health Visitor. I attended the local Child Guidance Clinic to discuss possibilities for Simon's education. I put on a great show of brightness and optimism, and entire reasonableness, which I now think convinced everyone how well I had accepted the situation. But I do not remember ever once talking about my, or my husband's feelings. Nor was I ever offered any help or advice in the management of this difficult child. Very likely I gave the impression that I did not need it. If only someone had probed just a little way below the surface . . . perhaps they, too, were afraid to stir up the powerful mixture of bitterness, rejection and failure that lay there.

I must have been very difficult to live with at this time. I cried very easily, and became very tense whenever I talked of Simon. My husband could not help me, nor I him, though we tried to adopt a united attitude. I did not want, as he did, to attend meetings of the National Society for Autistic Children, and he went off to them alone. I was rejecting relationships forced on me by a common misfortune, I told myself. In fact, I was still rejecting the misfortune. I preferred my happy, optimistic work for the National Childbirth Trust. I needed comfort. Even there, however, there was not much to be had. I could no longer join in the discussions about educational methods, for instance – they did not apply, or so I felt. No one really wanted to discuss educational facilities for the mentally handicapped. They might well be persuaded to listen to a talk on the subject, but they would not have views of their own to offer. They were not involved.

This phase of living on two levels lasted with me for several years. Its length could, I think, have been reduced with help and support, and the damage which it inflicted on our marriage might have been lessened. The "might have been" however, lies in the realm of conjecture. Today, I simply wish we had had some help. Help did come in the end, but not in the way I was expecting it, nor from the sources where I looked to find it, and it came too late to avert the catastrophes which still lay in the future. Fortunately, for me at least, I was still unsuspecting that there could be any trials ahead greater than those I was struggling to live with.

For, when it came to Simon himself, I had to learn about him, to get to know him, all over again. Having made the discovery that the child I loved was not the same as the child I thought I had loved, I had to sort out the confusion. The only way, then, that I could see of doing this was to banish at once the illusory child, the child-that-might-have-been, who had only ever existed in my and his father's imagination, whose success and talents were to have been a constant source of satisfaction and gratification – our stake in the future. This product of some sort of ego-projection was no longer relevant to our lives. The real child, the child I now held protectively in my arms, was never going to give us that sort of gratification. He had something to give us, something, perhaps, of greater price than anything our other children could offer, but we were not ready to see it then.

The act of banishment was harder than it had seemed on first taking the decision. It never was quite completed. Even now, Simon's ghost, as I call it, returns to haunt me a little from time to time, when I look at other, normal boys of his age and wonder what my tall son would have been like if ... It does not hurt me now, though – it grows a little thinner each year. It is only a shade, a nostalgia.

What then, who then was Simon, this child who had been born to travel far and light, as William Langland saw those like him, without our knowing? He was, symbolically, born on a Thursday. I did not know which star had presided at his birth, but it must have been a star of great ruthlessness, to produce a human being so beautiful, and so defenceless.

I did not, I realized now, know him at all in the sense that I had not the slightest idea how his mind worked. It was like watching a particularly complicated silent movie, without the help of sub-titles. He could not explain himself – he could not tell me anything beyond his immediate physical needs, and not always these. He smiled or laughed when he was happy – though sometimes he would burst out laughing for no apparent reason – and he would cry when hurt. Why he screamed I still did not know. I could see that certain groups of sensations caused him pleasure, and that these were mainly connected with the senses of taste and touch. The pleasure was obviously great, for he would linger over them, standing in the sea, perpetually licking the salt off his fingers, stroking the cat's fur, or his sister's newly washed hair. He loved motion, too, as he sat on the swing in the garden, but fortunately never to excess, as do many autistic children. Music, when it was structured and harmonious, delighted his ear, whereas the sound of engines or water frightened it. I have often wondered whether he heard some sounds more acutely than others. He did have audiometry tests, but it was impossible for these to be finely accurate as he was unable to communicate his reactions. I longed, as I still do long, for him to speak to me. The barrier, now that I realized its existence, seemed very cruel.

Somewhat feverishly, I turned to the experts to help me to get to know my own child, only to find that all they could do was point out patterns. I needed and tried to help, to do something positive. We cooperated with every test that was proposed, and there were plenty. I particularly remember a questionnaire from the University of California, then carrying out a research project upon autistic children, which took us some two hours to complete, and which included questions such as "did your grandmother rock her head in bed at night?" We took it seriously, and it *was* serious, out of such stray observations significant facts may emerge – but it did not all really help us to make contact with Simon. Perhaps it helped us to make a little more contact with ourselves. To get to know Simon, we had to live with him, as observantly, as sensitively, and as compassionately as possible, surround him with love, and, above all, expect nothing in return.

So far as he and I were concerned, it was this realization that helped us to be happier together. It was as if he felt me relax with him, as if he knew that I was no longer forcing him towards a normality he did not possess, wanting from him what he could not give me. He seemed to feel that, if anything, something had happened to make me love him more than ever.

I was very aware of his physical beauty, his one great, indisputable asset. It helped him with me. That may sound cynical, but beautiful things and people give me pleasure, daily pleasure. It is alas, much easier to want to help a beautiful handicapped child than to help a repulsively ugly or disfigured one. "Christ, he's beautiful!" exclaimed one long-haired Pimlico type photographer, feverishly twisting his camera lens to get a good close-up of Simon for a publicity picture for the Society, "can't you *see* how beautiful he is?" He could not know my feelings. "Yes," I replied simply, with a smile, "I do see it." But he never saw it as I did, the combination of almost perfect physical beauty with the absence of a personality that expresses itself in language ... the unutterable sadness of it.

He was a big, sturdy boy for his age. His skin was a clear brown – darker than the average Anglo-Saxon. His hair was thick and black, his features marvellously symmetrical. His eyes were brilliant, dark grey, fringed by long lashes. At times they would be alert, full of light and life. At others they would be dull, curiously unfocused, almost, it seemed, of a different shape. In the wide forehead, the delicate lines and curves of lips and chin, there was something that seemed to suggest that here, waiting, pleading with us to find the key and let it out, was intelligence. And there was something else, something infinitely gentle that roused me often to tears – I know now that it was total innocence. Time has proved me wrong about the first interpretation: Simon is not, and can never be, very intelligent. But it has proved me right about the second.

He has grown up into one of the gentlest of people – into someone who has, quite simply, none of the more tormented aspects of human nature. He cannot understand the concept of competition. He has never, in his life, tried to be first. He has never, ever, shown the least aggression towards any creature except in pure imitation (he loves to imitate, and does it excellently) of someone else's, such as my own. If you are deprived of language to the point where nothing abstract has any meaning for you, then you cannot make the fundamental choice of mankind between good and evil. No wonder Simon's face is often commented on for its serenity.

I realized, as I watched and listened to my friends with their children, that the relationship I wanted to create with Simon would have to be different from the average, and that I myself was going to have to change very considerably to meet its demands. In order to bring it about, I was going to have to stand aside from all the ordinary parental feelings with the exception of love. I am no saint, and I certainly had no intention of becoming a martyr, but I was very determined to build something out of all this ruin. That determination was Simon's only hope, and as I began to try to work on it, I met my first taste of happiness for a long time. For the first time I was loving him for what he was, and for what he might become, knowing that this could never be the same as other people. What I wanted for him was no longer normality, but a useful, dignified place in society.

Fortunately for me and my new ambitions, the care of Simon was not as difficult as it might have been, not half as strenuous as it is for the parents of many autistic children. My patience, and my physical endurance were never stretched to impracticable lengths. The Californian survey, conducted by the psychiatrist Bernard Rimland, had revealed, using the method known as cluster analysis, that Simon came into a sub-group of autistic children, who, whilst displaying the classic language disability, and many traits of autistic behaviour, are passive and docile. I have met many autistic children outside this group, and I know my luck. Nothing in our house was destroyed by Simon unless Joanna had incited him to the deed, with the exception of one pretty carriage clock, which for a reason he was never able to disclose Simon decided to stuff with chewed apple. It never recovered from this outrage and still stands in the sitting room, silent and reproachful, known to this day as the "apple clock". I don't think the clock repairer ever really believed me. Simon learned more slowly than average – but learn he did – to eat with reasonable manners, to dress and generally care for himself. I worked hard over the matter of manners and general social behaviour, because I wanted other people to find it easier to accept him. On the other hand, they had to discover, too, that too much could not be asked of him. We had to try and tread a delicate path of compromise.

His general health, too, was extremely good – the autism was uncomplicated by other handicaps. This, again, was fortunate, as medical treatment of an autistic child can be a painful business for both patient and doctor. He caught the usual childhood diseases, but never very badly. The only unusual feature of his physical health was the frequency of his nose bleeds, which seemed to happen for no reason at all. They were copious, and they frightened him, to the point where sedation became necessary. The only real difficulty, in fact, about caring for him physically, was in differentiating between real pain and mere discomfort: the screams were of the same pitch and volume for either. Again, we were lucky in that there was never any major illness to diagnose. He always seemed to be outraged by physical pain, as though disbelieving that there could exist anything so obviously removed from the correct order of things. He disliked getting dirty, although that is not a practice I discourage, and, once taught the rituals of personal hygiene, was able to carry them out. He loved new clothes – another minor blessing, for I have known the opposite be true – and would stand for ages admiring himself in front of the long mirror, while I had visions of him ending up as an artist's model.

These, however, are all superficialities, though they contributed to the texture of our lives. The person who was Simon remained an elusive mystery to me. He still does, and perhaps always will. I have come to think that it is not possible to know someone unless language (and by that I do not just mean speech) exists between you. I could not be sure that it ever would exist between Simon and me, or Simon and the rest of the world. To try to reach him, therefore, in his remoteness, we would have to try to find substitutes. They could never function as well as words, but they were better than making no contact at all. Making contact had become one of my chief aims in life.

It never occurred to me at the time to look at the change which had taken place in my scale of values. Human intelligence had toppled from its throne, and I had never even seen it go. Something else had taken its place, but I did not know it, and went my way with Simon blissfully unaware that my thoughts, words and deeds were under entirely new government. I knew I had come through a crisis, but I had assumed it to be, as it were, on a local level. I certainly had not the least idea of the implications, of the seemingly endless ramifications of that one, great, desperate and unconscious clutching at survival – for him, for my husband, for myself, for Joanna and for the two children yet to come.

3

A Place in the Family

As the months passed and we found, or so I thought, that we could still achieve some happiness together, despite the blow that had rocked our home to its foundations, the question of the size of our family raised its head once more. Providentially, Joanna had been born before any serious doubts about Simon's condition had crystallized, so that, by the time he was diagnosed, we had in her a living proof of our ability to have normal children. At just over two, she exuded intelligence, energy, mischief and, when it came to speech, we had the ingratitude to be grateful for the occasional respite when she fell asleep.

In the early days of our marriage, before Simon was conceived, we had often talked of having four children – three of our own, and the last one we would adopt. I have often been asked why we wanted to do this, but can only give the conscious reasons, which probably satisfy nobody. Just after we both left university, there was a great deal of racial disquiet in this country, with riots and senseless cruelties, which shocked and horrified us. I had had several Indian and African friends, and could not understand the prejudice that now acted against them. There seemed to be nothing that we could do as individuals that would affect the general scene. There was no solution we could offer that would put everything right. But solutions are not always quantitative. We felt that by adopting a child of mixed race we would create at least one small corner of society where this particular prejudice would not exist. It would be a very small gesture, but it would be better than no gesture at all. It would, we hoped,

31

be peaceful, and it would speak more eloquently than words. We both, or so I thought, felt very strongly about it.

Simon's diagnosis, however, had made the realization of these early dreams very dubious indeed. During the first period of shock, they were forgotten altogether. Gradually, however, I began to experience an ever more intense desire for a third baby of our own. It grew from an almost inevitable sense of having failed my husband. Whilst I was quickly sure that I could accept Simon's handicapped state for myself, I was by no means certain that I could accept it for him. Nor was I sure that he accepted it, though outwardly he seemed to do so. I wanted to give him a normal son; I needed to do so. It seemed to me the natural way of healing a hurt such as we had sustained, just as one recovers fully from a miscarriage once a new pregnancy begins. The intensity of the need revealed itself in a three month false pregnancy, missed periods, morning sickness and all, and fortified itself with a three month miscarriage. Fortune, it seemed, was never going to smile our way again. The next pregnancy, however, stayed put, with the help of weekly injections.

It was a traumatic time. I was fully aware of all the risks we were taking, of all that could go wrong. I was thirty-three – no longer the best age for child-bearing, the age when the incidence of mental handicap begins to creep up. My doctor had his own fears about the effects of the injections. The thalidomide scare was still fresh in everyone's minds. Could we survive if I bore another handicapped child? The question had no answer. We could only wait and see. If only I had felt less tired, less ill – it was a long, long nine months ...

The birth of Tom, huge, lusty nine pound Tom, did everything at once. It restored my faith in us as a family, in myself as a mother, and in our capacity for happiness. I had desperately wanted the baby to be a boy, and my wishes were granted – here he was. The luck, it seemed, had turned. I had no way, there and then, of being sure he was normal – I no longer trusted his good looks – but he certainly was not mongoloid, my chief fear, and his face, as he fed, wore the same expression of concentration as Joanna's once had. I was sure inside myself that all was well. I watched out for the milestones of development, but with no real anxiety. I was experienced now, and knew what I was looking for. When babbling, the prelude to speech, began, I could rejoice. Simon had never babbled. Sure enough, in due and proper time, speech developed, bringing with it proofs of imagination and intelligence. Tom was fine.

Tom healed me. He removed, probably for ever, the traces of guilt and bitterness which might have marred my relationship with Simon. His presence and needs prevented me from devoting myself too claustrophobically to Simon, forcing me to spread the distribution of love and anxiety. He also gave something special to Simon.

Simon was five and a half at the time of Tom's birth. He had already begun to attend school – of a kind – and was beginning to improve a little in his tolerance of other people. He was still difficult to manage, but we were learning fast how to woo him into more acceptable ways of behaviour.

Some of the changes in him were apparent when he was brought in to see his new baby brother for the first time. After the lovely experience of Joanna's birth, I had once again elected to have the baby at home. I occupied a temporary bedroom on the ground floor, and, as in the previous confinement, was up and about for much of the first stage of labour. We had once again engaged a temporary nannie, as the last experiment had worked out so well. Jeannette had gone off to a job in the States, but Anne from Northumberland turned out to be even more successful, and was not a wit dismayed at having to cope single-handed with an autistic child and a lively three year old. Tom, with a love of precision which is a definite characteristic of his temperament, decided to arrive on the exact day that he was due, and made his home run exactly at tea-time, which remains his favourite meal. The other two, consuming fresh-baked scones in the kitchen with Anne, heard his first cry.

I shall never forget their solemn faces when, a short time later, she brought them in to see who had arrived. I watched Simon, remembering his chilling indifference to the advent of his sister.

This time, there was no trace of indifference. It was all quite different. The sight of Tom, red, wrinkled and snuffling like a piglet in his warm white shawl awoke some hitherto dormant emotion in Simon. He was visibly moved. He advanced to look into the crib, while I sat on my hands to prevent any defensive gesture. "Baby," he murmured, and again, "Baby." "Baby Tom," I told him, "your new brother." "Your new brother," he echoed, as he always did, unable to take his eyes off this marvel. I held my breath as he put out his hand, and stroked the baby's silky head, very, very gently. Then he smiled. I cried.

After that it was hard to keep Simon out of the room. No one could accuse him of indifference this time. He didn't want to miss anything. Fearfully at first, but with increasing confidence, we allowed him to help – with dusting, and drying, and folding and poppers. Tom was a calm, easy-going baby, except when he was hungry. Before long, seated well in the middle of the bed – just in case – Simon was allowed to hold him. We felt sure he understood the privilege.

It was Joanna who was the least anxious to join the adoring throng. She was interested in the baby for a time, but the novelty quickly wore off, and, in any case, she was wildly jealous. We tried to include her in the baby rituals, but she was not having any. She gave play to her maternal feelings by wrapping every cuddly toy in the house in my new nappies, and put one on the cat, for good measure. She consented to draw the new baby for me, and presented me with a very creditable portrait of a caterpillar. I revelled in these reactions. I was learning with Joanna all that I had missed learning with Simon.

Tom grew fast. By the time he was nearly two, he was a big, heavy toddler with angelic, fair features, angelic fair hair and blue eyes, and a daemonic will of his own, which fairly staggered me. He had not yet started to scream, at which art he was to put up a very fair imitation of his elder brother, but he had discovered the invaluable weapon of sulking. He was so stubborn that he often won when he should not have done, but at least he left me in no doubt: he was a whole, complex personality, and as yet there was nothing more to worry about than that it demanded of me a degree of diplomacy comparable with that required at Summit Conferences.

We settled down once again to the business of integration as a family. I thought we were making a fair success of it. The older Simon grew, the more his behaviour improved. Many of his anti-social characteristics fell away, including the screaming, which gradually diminished in ferocity. New, odd quirks would crop up for a while – such as his passion for collecting bits of plastic, and carrying one around in his mouth – only to die in their turn. He lost his fear of the barber and the dentist, and came to regard both experiences as something of a treat. The local dental hospital had recommended us to an excellent local dentist who agreed to treat Simon, and who, over the years, has successfully built up a relationship of trust and confidence with him, so that he can even put small fillings in second teeth when necessary. Our dentist recommended painting Simon's teeth with fluoride, to stave off lesions as long as possible as he is not sure whether he could instal a big filling without a general anaesthetic. Both the dentist and myself tried to obtain this highly successful preventive treatment on the National Health Service, on the grounds of Simon's handicap, and the distress it was likely to save him, but it proved impossible. I have to pay a large sum of money every six months to renew the fluoride – yet the general anaesthetic would cost the Health Service more.

His relationship with Tom remained good. He loved to repeat everything I said to him, be it polite or not, in tones that exactly matched my own. He was growing positively maternal.

I felt, and I thought that we felt, that we had been entirely justified in having this third child, from the point of view of each member of the family. Simon, growing up amidst other children, would be obliged to acquire some of the art of sharing his life with them, as well, as having the help, as he grew older, of loving and loyal supporters. Whilst we firmly believed that it did not hurt Joanna to grow up alongside a handicapped brother, it was nonetheless better for her that she should also have a normal sibling in whom to confide, and with whom she could enjoy a normal brother-sister relationship. And it was better for us as parents, I thought, that we could be more completely normal parents, as well as the parents of an autistic child.

This train of thought led, insidiously, to the resurrection of that old dream of adopting a fourth child. We discussed the possibilities, trying to view the matter from all sides. Try as we might, we could not see how the presence of a child such as Simon in our midst should automatically exclude us from the ranks of possible adopters. We had, we felt, already overcome the main difficulties of learning to live with him. We had, indeed, come to look on living with him as giving our normal children a position of privilege. From him they could learn, far better than from ourselves or from teachers, lessons of tolerance and compassion which otherwise they might never absorb. They would never be afraid, as I had been, of mentally handicapped people. Joanna, in fact, had already gone to the opposite extreme – she was passionately protective towards him. Too much so just then, for his or her good – she tended to treat him like a beloved but rather obtuse Labrador, and talk down to him in a tone whose superiority set my teeth on edge. This did not worry me too much, however: it could be modified later. Basically, it was going in the right direction.

Surely, therefore, if we regarded living with Simon as good for our own children, it could not be bad for an adopted child. As the strange child came to grow up with our own, would not he or she, too, come to love Simon, taking his cue from the rest of the family, and be permanently enriched by that love? So I believed, so I believed passionately. My husband seemed to agree, and I was too blinded by my own enthusiasm to notice any lack of conviction in his agreement, any flaw in my own arguments. I contacted the local adoption society, and put the case to them. We wanted, I explained, to adopt a baby of mixed race, preferably a girl – a baby who was perhaps difficult to place. (At that time it was much harder to adopt such babies than it is now.)

The result was a plethora of visits, nearly always occurring at high-pressure times, such as meals, or bath. We were asked reams of questions about our motives for wishing to adopt, about our attitude to Simon, about our respective families, which we did our best to answer. We were interviewed both together and separately, so that each might answer uninhibited by the presence of the other. We must have passed muster, as we were accepted as potential adoptive parents. No one else, it seems, had picked up that lack of conviction in my husband, either. My enthusiasm blinded us all.

Nine months later, we all drove off to fetch home our nutbrown David from his foster home. He sat on my lap in the car, staring at me with troubled, puzzled, eyes. Who was I? Who indeed? – he had no possible way of telling. That worried look of his went straight to my heart. I longed to smooth it away, but I knew only months of love and patience could do that. He solved the present difficult situation as best he could, by falling asleep. It was the simplest way out. We all needed time.

David's coming caused Simon some uneasy moments. He was perplexed and suspicious about the new arrival. David was no silky haired bundle, wrapped in shawls, but a vastly energetic and sociable individual, who learned to crawl with speed, accuracy and determination within a week of entering the family, clutching people and objects alike en route with strong, monkey fingers. Simon found himself being pinched, pulled and generally used as a babywalker in a way he had never been called upon to tolerate before, from either Tom or Joanna. Generally he reacted by shoving David off, somewhat half-heartedly, with an impatient grunt.

But David was a baby and a half. He had a will and a way, capable as he was of immense spurts of energy which would suddenly die down like a turned-off fountain, leaving him asleep. His enormous, delighted smile was then his outstanding characteristic, and he directed the full blast of it at Simon, making it quite clear that he liked him, homing in on him ruthlessly every time he set eyes on him. I think that he sensed Simon's fundamental peacefulness of temperament, and derived comfort from it. He interpreted the impatient shoves, which were, incidentally, never strong enough to hurt, as a new game, and returned for more of the same treatment, beaming and chuckling. Well, beaming and chuckling are very basic forms of communication, and Simon received the message loud and clear. He beamed and chuckled back. A great new friendship was born.

Simon seemed to realize that he had advantages of size and strength, despite David's increasing agility. He never knowingly hurt him. If anything, he was protective towards him, as he was towards Tom, though with the latter the experience was less rewarding. The advent of a nine month old adoptive brother had proved a traumatic experience for poor Tom. He still had not sufficient speech to express himself verbally, and rushed instead into a tantrum stage which in duration and vigour was to rival his autistic brother's. For a solid year, whenever any of my friends phoned me and heard him screaming in the background, she would ask automatically, "Is that Tom?" And it always was.

Gradually he grew out of it, and began to come to terms with David, but it took a long time. Tom is a very artistic child, and as he began to express himself more in colour, in music and in writing, so he came to achieve some control of his feelings. Today, I can smile. Tom and David are devoted to each other. They fight like puppies, but their affection is visible, and it is possible to see how much each has helped the other.

Joanna's feelings were also mixed. She was very proud of her new little brother, and insisted on my taking him along when I went to meet her from school, to be displayed to all her friends, but she was highly irritated by his exuberant energy. She was jealous, too, and I suspect that many a poke was delivered behind my back. Nowadays, whilst she still is liable to be irritated by the same excess of zeal, she acknowledges the effervescence he has brought into the family, and nearly always takes his part when my wrath is about to explode over his curly head.

In those days, however, it was definitely with Simon that David had the easiest time. Small wonder that he turned to him. And Simon retained his tolerance towards this increasingly rumbustious member of the family, who contrived to bring out whatever embryonic elements of authority, of assertion that lay hidden amongst his general passiveness. "Stop it, David," I have heard him bellow, convulsed with laughter at his own daring, "Naughty David. Stop it *now!*"

Those who doubted our wisdom in adopting a fourth child when we already had a handicapped child in the family should have heard that. In the event, they were to prove right, of course, but not for the reasons they would then have given, if pressed. Usually, they contented themselves with saying how "brave" we were – which meant, of course, how mad. I think also they questioned the genuineness of our charity in bringing a baby into a family where, love or no love, it would inherit some of the burden that, in the long term, the responsibility for Simon must prove to be.

Such a criticism cannot be dismissed lightly. However one may argue the point, we were not, despite the mildness of Simon's particular form of handicap, despite our apparent good adjustment to the blow, a normal family. We were a family under stress, and I, for one, completely underestimated that stress, totally blind to all its infinite ramifications. Stress, I think now, is like ground elder – the least bit overlooked is capable of producing an entirely new network of roots. When we decided to take on David, I thought that we had successfully worked our way through the main problems. We loved, accepted and respected our mentally handicapped son, and were capable of teaching our normal children to do the same. We had, I thought, successfully banished the guilt, the disappointment, the frustration from our lives. I was very naïve. Such feelings do not respond to arbitrary attack in that way. It merely drives them underground, where they flourish, and become far more dangerous. This happened in our case, though I did not know it, and went on blissfully with my job of building up and maintaining family life, totally unaware of what was happening underneath, in the foundations. To this extent, our friends were right.

They were right, too, in another way. Parents have a frightening tendency, if one child "fails" them, as ours had done, to transfer all the disappointed hopes and expectations onto the other children. This is, I think, one of the heaviest burdens that siblings of a mentally handicapped child have to carry. Few outsiders recognize its weight.

We were aware of this danger, but even so I am sure that Joanna, at least, has suffered from it. She has, of all the family, paid the heaviest price. Chronologically, she is the second child, yet in mental ability, in sensitivity – in every other way – she is the eldest. Instinctively she looked up to her elder brother, only to find that the leadership had inexplicably devolved upon her. This in itself is a disturbing disruption of the norm for a small child to accept, and I think that the struggle to do so has left its mark upon her. I tried hard not to expect too much of her, but I do not think I understood all the implications of her position clearly enough. People today often remark on Joanna's maturity of outlook, and are sometimes irritated by the precocity of her comments. They do not always pause to consider that it was Joanna who co-existed with Simon's reign of terror and her parents' grief, Joanna who witnessed the weird behaviour, and who was deafened by the screaming, Joanna who learned far, far earlier than most people what it means – exactly – to be mentally handicapped. Few friends, fewer teachers, have ever realized just how much support Joanna needed.

The two little brothers suffered less, in that by the time they were old enough to be aware of it, the worst of the autistic behaviour had disappeared into the kindly realms of memory. There is still a disruption of the norm, but they, at least, have Joanna's lead to follow. To them, in everything but size, Joanna is the eldest of the children. If I do expect more of them, at least I try to catch myself at it, and stop in time. I do not want to magnify this danger of transference of expectations. It exists, and it is well to be aware of it, but it exists in other, "normal" families as well – where one child, perhaps the eldest, is merely less bright than the rest of the family.

I think that if we had been given more support around the time of the adoption, many of our actual and incipient difficulties might have been brought to light, and smoothed away. As soon as the adoption was made final in the court, the visitors vanished. Their job, they evidently thought, was done. They had handed it over to us. We, like all other parents, must learn to know and rear the new baby by ourselves. But we were not like other parents, and, in any case, adoption is not a natural process. I do not think that parents, especially those with children of their own, should always, as a rule, be left to get on with it. Love for the adopted baby does not always appear instantly – however great it may grow with time – and the mixed and perhaps violent feelings of the natural children in the adoptive family may well prove too complicated for the parents to deal with. They were, for a while, in our case. I wondered again and again if Tom was going to make himself autistic through sheer negativism of his temperament. It was a very difficult time for me, and I longed to have someone to talk to, someone who could understand my problems and put them in perspective, who might help me in guiding the children. For at that time – the months after the adoption – there was, in fact, no one. When the crisis I had not anticipated burst upon me, a few months later, I was feeling more isolated – amid many friends – than I had ever felt before.

Life with the children, however, had to go on, to develop, despite my anxieties. We tried to live it from day to day, without too much worried looking ahead. There was no support, and we had to manage as best we could. The children had to learn to accept each other, and we had to learn how to form their widely differing and contrasting personalities into a harmonious ensemble. I was fast discovering how, in dealing with Simon, they quickly took their cue from me, at least in their early days. If they brought friends home to tea and Simon treated us to a display of his more eccentric behaviour, it was my calm, my appearance of perfect acceptance, that helped them through, whatever any of us were feeling inside.

I had one golden rule: no one, but no one, ever laughed *at* Simon in our house, or indeed, in our presence. I explained his difficulties to the children's friends as simply as possible, just as I had in my own family. They were often very puzzled. They often did not understand. But they could always understand that he needed their help – and they never failed to respond to that. One little girl asked me if Simon would ever get better, and when (I don't believe in mincing the truth), I told her that, though he might one day speak a little more, he would never be able to be like her, she burst into tears. Those children did a good deal to restore my faith in humanity, which by that time was wearing rather thin.

There came the day, however, when Joanna was seven or eight, when she began to be embarrassed by her brother's behaviour. She desperately wanted us to conform. By this time, he was nine or ten, his behaviour was infinitely less eccentric than it had been when he was small, but he could not satisfy Joanna's herd instinct. I can remember the day when we were waiting in the shoe shop, and she implored me, in an agonized whisper, to "please tell Simon to stop making his sawing noise". He was only quietly running through, to himself, his splendid imitation of a branch being sawn off a tree, with a satisfying clunk at the end as it fell to the ground, and I was rather enjoying it, but I saw her real distress, and quickly shushed him. I wondered how to help her through this embarrassment, which was going to give her a good deal of pain, and found the answer in appealing to her sense of humour – which is, perhaps as a result, very well developed. My own is of the kind which delights in incongruous situations, and Simon has kept me well supplied with these. I pointed out to Joanna how comical people can look when they are confronted by a situation which is out of the ordinary –

the outrage on the face of the strange lady in the super-
market, for instance, when Simon strokes her fur collar, a
rapturous expression on his face, saying "Pussy" – or, better
still, the supreme embarrassment of young men when the
beards they so proudly sport suffer the same treatment. She
responded enthusiastically and has learned to enjoy the observation of personality which such situations afford. Adolescent
now, I do not think she is ever embarrassed by her tall brother,
but is quite devoted to him, ever ready to help him, to explain
for him, to make his path easier.

The little boys, now seven and nine themselves, do not seem
to feel this embarrassment. Their big brother is now threatening to pass the six foot mark, and in any case commands
their support through sheer size. His gentleness, his amiability,
his slowness of pace are an oasis of stillness in all the hurrying,
skirmishing and fretting of family life. They include him in
their games whenever possible, and if I hear them at times
"acting superior" it only needs the smallest reminder from me
that, while they were lucky enough to enter the world un-
scathed, Simon wasn't. They accept the lesson, and do their
best to make amends. They love him, and miss him when he is
away from home.

I have noticed with joy their growing solicitude for other
handicapped children. Tom came home from school furiously
indignant because his mates had been shouting "spastic" as a
term of abuse. He knew what the word really meant. I think
he could well be a good influence on his friends.

David, too, in learning to help with Simon's handicap learns
to deal with his own. Being adopted and coloured in a white
family is not a situation conducive to a strong feeling of
security. Again, a growing sense of humour helps him
to take the name-calling as a joke, and the family imagination,
pooled, provides him with a stock of suitable epithets to offer
in return. Simon's example helps to give him a sense of proportion, which may avert bitterness as he grows older. He has
never seen Simon angry. Whilst I cannot deny that he has
to share part of a load, in being Simon's youngest brother, I
do not think that sharing such a load works to his detriment,
but rather to his good.

It has been the sharing out of my attention and support that
has proved the biggest difficulty, and one which I feel can

never be solved to perfection. Every parent feels this to some extent, but where there is a handicapped child the problem is rather bigger. I have always felt very strongly that, if humanly possible, the normal children must not be sacrificed to the handicapped one, despite the special needs. Attention must be divided into equal shares. Of course, I have never succeeded in living up to this ideal – all sorts of things, such as accident, or illness, or family crisis, can upset the balance. I have felt, nonetheless, that it is an ideal worth striving for, if each, including Simon, was to achieve real maturity. Nothing I could do, nothing I could teach him, would make Simon normal – the teaching I did undertake with him was to help us both, to enable us to make better contact with each other – therefore it would not have been right to sacrifice the others, who each, also, had a life in front of him or her. Nor would it have given Simon a genuine experience of family life.

I was no longer struggling to make him normal. My aims had changed: I wanted now to open up his limited life to its fullest possible extent, that he should know the experience of human love, in its widest sense, and learn to give what he could, as well as to receive. If I could help bring all this about for him, his years of life, however poverty stricken in some respects, need not be altogether insignificant.

4

The Bridge of Words

Within the problem of sharing out attention fairly between the children lay concealed a basic difficulty which had to be looked at very objectively, and which, in fact, only increasing experience could help us to solve.

It is hard enough to share out the attention between normal children, who each have immensely varying temperaments and emotional needs. But at least with such children there is the common factor which makes it all approximately possible: you can communicate with them. They can express their pleasure or their dissatisfaction. "It isn't fair" is one of the plaints most often, and perhaps most resentfully heard in any family with two or more children. You may explode with righteous wrath, you may argue or explain, you may even reflect that the child has a grain of justice in his or her outcry – but at all events the child itself is capable of taking a hand in the matter.

This is simply not so of the passive autistic child. Simon has never in his life said "It isn't fair", because he has no grasp whatsoever of the abstract concept of justice, any more than he has on that of competition, or politics, or the international monetary system. It took a very long time for the full implications of the fact that abstractions are meaningless to him to dawn on me. When I first knew that he was autistic, I simply understood that he could not use language normally. Perhaps mercifully, I did not appreciate to what extent this was to cut him off from the rest of human kind. Using language does not, as I thought then, mean just using meaningful speech. It means formulating and expressing thoughts and feelings so that they can be understood by others. Language includes gesture and facial expression – as in mime. The deaf, the blind and the dumb can be taught, although with difficulty, to formulate, express and understand language, with the help of substitutes such as Braille and hand signs – enough at least to help them to participate to a reasonable extent in the life of the community around them. This is not so of the autistic. The substitutes for language are as meaningless to them, unless they receive special training, as is language itself. The whole machine is unsynchronized – not just one part of it. Some autistic children remain mute for the whole of their lives. Others, more fortunate, do develop a degree of meaningful speech. Still others can become positively garrulous, yet the speech is still not that of "normal" people – it is frequently stereotyped, rigid, confined to one topic which is of obsessive interest to them, and which is embarked on with enthusiasm regardless of its relevance, or of the interest, or lack of it, of the audience. It is a far cry from the marvellous flexibility of human language at its most developed – though I cannot help thinking that it is perhaps not so far removed from the perorations of some elderly professors, sunk in their specialities, regardless of their captive audience.

Where Simon was concerned, we had a very basic problem. He was not able to claim my attention with words, nor that of anyone else. The onus was therefore entirely on us to come to him in his isolation, and to help him develop means of escaping from it. He had some speech, but it was very, very little, in comparison with, for instance, Joanna. I could only get through to him by using simple commands reinforced by physical compulsion, and he could only get through to me by laughing, screaming, reciting poems or by taking me by the hand and leading me to whatever he wanted. It did not seem much to go on. I was puzzled, and very, very frustrated. I had no idea how to set about bridging the frightening gap between us. I did not know how to play with him other than in purely physical romping, how to interest him in any creative, learning activity which would, in itself, bring us closer together, forge a bond between us, and I was finding the experience of feeling totally cut off from him, as he grew, unendurable. I wanted to give him the time and attention that it was so easy to give Joanna, but I had no idea how to use them.

There was no professional guidance. No expert ever suggested anything at all. I was on my own, for all the world as if the problem did not exist. It was entirely by coincidence – one of those coincidences that have happened too regularly along Simon's path for them really to justify the name – that one of my friends passed over to me an article which she had cut from an educational magazine. It was a review of a book entitled, *Teach Your Baby to Read*, by Glenn Doman, an American psychiatrist. The message of this book is that very young children, as young as two years and under, can be taught by their parents to enjoy reading, and, indeed, to read fluently long before they reach school age. The method advocated is basically "Look-Say", but substituting giant flash cards with red print for the smaller ones usually used, to help the less developed eye of the infant, and suggesting a system of reward by effusive, though variable praise to act as a stimulus.

I bought the book, read it carefully, and thought about it a great deal. This was just at the time of Simon's diagnosis. He was four, and Joanna was two.

Obviously, there was no point in trying to teach him to read when he could not speak more than a few disconnected words and phrases. But I wondered if, by trying to teach him to read words, if not phrases and sentences, aloud, by dint of harnessing this extraordinary mechanical memory of his, I might not be able to accustom him at least to enjoying the use of words, the saying of them, to create, as it were, a habit. There certainly did not seem to be much to lose by trying. Other than his few spontaneous words, the rest of his speech was entirely echolalic – he merely repeated the last words of the sentence addressed to him, with a hopeful look as if to say "Was that what you wanted me to say?". "Shall we go to the shops?" would produce the response "Go to the shops?" I never knew whether he actually *wanted* to. If we could only improve on this a little, we would have achieved something.

The idea, in all its simplicity, certainly appealed to me more than another kind of therapy much publicized at that time in the media, known as "operant conditioning", a technique which also employed reward and punishment for appropriate and inappropriate behaviour. It was the type of reward and punishment which revolted me – the appeasement of hunger, or the deprivation of light, for instance – which struck me as insulting the basic humanity of the child, every bit as much as brain washing or torture. I did not want to walk that bridge to Simon, if bridge it could be called. I wanted his trust, not his fear. I wanted to woo him into joining the rest of us, not capture him by force.

So, very naïvely, blind to the magnitude of the task ahead, we started. I cut out the first giant flash cards, and painted on the thick red letters. "Mummy" and "Daddy" were the first two pawns to advance. As he never spoke either word very clearly, even if we stopped right there we would have something on the credit side. But we did not stop there. Within a few days he could recognize either word, and say it aloud. I found myself busily cutting out the dozen or so smaller cards that formed the next move. These were all nouns, all denoting parts of the body so that they were easy to demonstrate. Our doctor, I reflected, would have reason to be grateful to Glenn Doman if ever Simon learned to say the name of the place where the pain was. I followed the book's instructions to the letter, and raised the roof with cries of glee every time he recognized a word and said it correctly. I insisted on correct pronunciation, as he was inclined to be sloppy in his articulation. By "insist", I do not mean that I sounded like a sergeant major. There was never any anger or harshness in our reading sessions. If a word was difficult for him to say – such as any word containing double consonants – I split it down into syllables, and, with the help of pulling funny faces, persuaded him to say it after me slowly until he could do it correctly, despite the giggles that convulsed him. Such reading methods are not for the inhibited! Anyone coming unexpectedly into the middle of one would have thought me completely crazy as I leaped around the room clutching an elbow, an eye or an ear bellowing "eye" – "that's right – JOLLY GOOD SIMON!" – while he came galloping after me, his face one great beam of delight.

It did not take very long for me to discover that he revelled in praise, and never failed to respond to it by renewed efforts. It made me realize that he had experienced all too little of it during his short life. As we progressed, I did my best to follow Glenn Doman's advice and space it out at variable intervals, so that it did not inevitably follow success, which might have become boring in the long run. But the book had not been written as a therapy for autistic children, with their love of sameness, and Simon foiled this attempt at increasing the stimulus by supplying the praise for himself if I failed to come up with it. "Jolly good Simon" he would exclaim, with a seraphic beam, if I agreed that he had duly recognized the word but was not doing anything about it. And there was nothing for it but to agree, if it gave him that much pleasure. I could not foresee that I might be making things difficult for his future teachers by allowing him to become over-dependent on praise. Even if I had, I doubt whether I would have changed my methods. There was, after all, no one to show me any better way, if one existed, and I could feel that through this new teaching-learning relationship we were coming into contact with each other. That, after all, was my chief aim. I was not looking further ahead. There had to be one solid relationship in his life on which he could build before he could turn out to the rest of the world and estab-lish others. I was sure of this. And until we began our reading "game" I had not felt that it existed. I had fed, clothed, cleaned, cuddled and romped with him, but that was not enough. We had to be able to talk to each other, however simply, and now we were beginning to do it.

Within a couple of weeks, to my great delight, he learned to recognize and say all the body words, touching the relevant part of his body as he did so, whatever the order in which they were presented to him. I began to realize that we could go much further than I had ever thought possible, and began to keep a diary, noting his progress. Another batch of cards was now necessary, smaller again, and this time in black ink, to prepare for the transition to ordinary type. The next group of words included verbs, conjunctions and pronouns. The verbs presented no difficulty – we ran, skipped, hopped, laughed and cried with gusto and comprehension. It was the pronouns and conjunctions which gave me my first taste of the dif-ficulties which faced us. I could think of no way of making them comprehensible. After several false attempts, I decided to let him simply learn them parrot fashion, and hope that the comprehension would eventually follow. I did the same with abstract adjectives and adverbs, and all conjunctions. Prepositions were more approachable, though he found them confusing, and we had to spend a lot of time with some of them.

This may give the impression that we spent hours each day over the reading sessions. This was not the case. I kept them very short indeed, starting with a mere five minutes each day, after lunch, when Joanna was having her rest and Simon could have my undivided attention. At the least sign of boredom or reluctance, I put the flash cards away. This was first and foremost a game, something he enjoyed doing, not something I was forcing him to do. I did not, in point of fact, put them away very often.

After a few weeks, however, matters became more complicated because Joanna, probably scenting that she was missing out on something, decided to give up her afternoon rest. I found I could not concentrate on Simon if she was screaming blue murder upstairs, so in the end, reluctantly, I had to let her stay up and join in. He did not appear to mind in the least, but I minded for him. Joanna already demanded, and received, a good deal of attention. It seemed unfair that she should now claim this as well. But she left me no choice. She saw that Simon was having fun, and she did not like being excluded. Weakly, I caved in, and began to show her the flash cards as well ... I thought she would soon tire of it – which shows that I did not know Joanna very well, either. I did not notice the determination in her eye. Quickly, she set about catching up with her brother.

The pile of cards that the children could recognize grew thicker and thicker. It was easy to drop them, muddle them, lose them altogether. It was also easier to let the level of excitement, the feeling of discovery, drop and fade. If interest was to be maintained, I felt we had to keep moving. I put away the piles of little cards. It was time to try for sentences.

At this point I put away the book, too. From now on, I felt I wanted to gear things to our particular needs. If Simon was to read and understand the best part of a number of sentences, I wanted them to be relevant to his daily life, to his needs. I wanted them to be sentences that he heard every day, or nearly every day, so that, having "learned" them, through reading, and heard them from other people, he might perhaps be tempted into trying them out for himself, at a relevant time and place. "I want to go to the lavatory" took pride of place, along with all the politeness formulae which would help make him more acceptable to other people. Before showing him the sentence, I checked that he could recognize each individual word that it contained by itself.

Deciphering the first sentence was an exciting moment. At first they read each word separately, without realizing the relationships they bore to each other, and, of course, they read slowly. We speeded it up – and suddenly, in Joanna's case first – light dawned. She saw the pattern. Simon echoed her, a little puzzled by the transformation of the hitherto simple game. It was, I saw, essential at this point to separate them. Joanna was ready to take off into realms where Simon could not hope to follow her, and, what is more, needed far less help, young as she was. I found I was spending a lot of time making up and writing out special sentences. What is more, I was enjoying it.

In time, however, this, too, became somewhat impracticable. The sentences were on long strips of card. They tore easily, and the favourites became grubby and stained. It was time, I decided, greatly daring, to adventure into our first reader. Books, after all, had not come by their present shape and form by accident.

The Ladybird series I found excellent for our purpose, with their clear, graduated type, clever system of repetition of key words, and sharp, bright pictures illustrating the reading material. From my own point of view I found them deadly dull, and fearfully middle-class, but the children liked them, and that was the main point. Simon, what is more, seemed to sense that reading a real book meant promotion, and put even more enthusiasm into his attempts to recognize the words. His memory, as I had hoped it would, rose to the demands made upon it. He rarely forgot words that he had once learned to distinguish, even if the reading sessions were dropped for some days, for one reason or another. His pleasure was apparent in his face, rather than in his voice. He always read, and still does, with entire monotony – another of the limitations I had to learn to recognize as un-stretchable.

Once we were reading books, Joanna became far less of a nuisance. She was by now hooked on the wonderful adventure of exploring this new world, and needed very little guidance. She no longer needed to compete with her brother, but seemed to feel the need to help him, infecting him with her own enthusiasm. I did not aim at perfection with her any more than I did with Simon. When either read to me we rarely repeated a page, but advanced always, making fresh discoveries all the time. I did correct mistakes, but I never let hesitations or "dry-ups" worry anybody – I cheated shamelessly, dropping hints, whispering syllables, or in the end perhaps the recalcitrant word itself. It was their interest I was after, the desire to go on, to find out, to dare ... And always, always, there was praise.

If the children's pleasure was to be the gauge of the success of the project, I still have no doubt that this success was total. They both loved reading. But there was more to it than that. I was reaping the rich reward of seeing Simon slowly, hesitantly, but with increasing confidence, make his way through his reader, all the time becoming more familiar with words.

I feel certain that any teacher reading this would stop me here, and say, "Ah! but don't you see – he's not really reading. His comprehension is only about sixty per cent – the rest is just the mechanical recognition of visual patterns." Later on, several teachers did indeed say that to me.

This criticism is perfectly accurate, but it totally misses the point of what I was trying to do. For me, teaching Simon to read was a means to an end, not an end in itself. I was trying to accustom him to saying words, whilst understanding as many of their meanings as possible – no more. If we incidentally achieved more than this, so much the better, but it was not the actual target. I was never, ever, trying to demonstrate his "normal" mental ability – I knew that we could not do that, for it did not exist. That would have implied that I had not accepted the incurable nature of his handicap, whereas I had, once I knew what it was. I found that other people were curiously unable to believe that I could wish to spend time and energy developing all the potential that lay *within the limits* of the handicap, whilst fully accepting the existence of those limits. I had been tremendously encouraged by meeting a young woman who, though obviously Mongoloid from the tell-tale cast of her features, was able, thanks to years of devoted work on the part of the family nannie, to converse fluently, and with considerable charm, about her work and her life in the family, and who was an acknowledged genius at crossword puzzles. She was so thoroughly nice I wanted to be friends with her. And it was her kind of achievement that I wanted for Simon, her kind of enjoyment of what life had to offer.

Thus, the fact that his "reading" soon began to outstrip his spontaneous speech was to me something that was absolutely to be expected. What I was waiting for, hoping for, ready to pounce upon was the overflow, as it were, from the full tank to the nearly empty one. And spasmodically, in the tiniest, most modest of trickles, it was beginning to happen as experience taught him that he could get what he wanted far more easily by trying out words than by screaming, and probably with an extra measure of the morale-cheering praise into the bargain.

He was not really learning to use language. Language is alive and flexible, able to convey the subtlest shades of emotion, the darkest depths of feeling, the uplifting of elation, all different in every human individual. I could not give him this priceless skill alive with its muscles and tendons, blood and viscera – I could only give him a few dead bones, rigid, as full of feeling as the Latin verbs in the grammar book. He had not the power to change them, to give them life. His stock of phrases remained in his mind exactly as they were printed in the reading book, and that was how he would use them always. When he brought them out in speech, with tenses, pronouns and adverbs all at odds with the actual situation, I could often identify the page where he had learned them.

In fact I can still remember the first day this happened, so great was our delight. We were nearing the end of a long, slow winter's walk (walks with Simon were always slow as he could never see the point of going fast) and the car was in sight. Suddenly, he petrified us by announcing, "Now it's time to go home." I recognized the phrase at once – it came near the end of the current Ladybird reader – but now, for the first time, he was using it, and above all, using it relevantly. We went home jubilant. Even if he only ever acquired the bones of language, they were better than no language at all. They could be used to build a bridge, just as some of those Latin verbs could be used to make some sort of contact with an Ancient Roman, found wandering forlornly up the M1.

All the same, our jubilation proved that we still did not

understand very much about the handicap. To us then, Simon's problems seemed capable of step by step, logical resolution. Once set upon the path of progress, we reasoned, he would, with adequate teaching, continue along it until he reached his limits, whatever they might turn out to be. But it did not work out like that. We waited for more spontaneous phrases to appear, brought out into daily use. And around that time quite a few did, encouraging our optimism – but only, some time later, inexplicably to vanish again. As he grew older, I began to realize that there was to be no pattern to his development, at least, to his mental development. The same was true of his social behaviour. He suddenly lost all fear of the washing machine noises, only to be instead terrified by the hitherto inoffensive pop of the central heating boiler. He stopped being obsessed by the buzz of friction toys, only to develop an inordinate passion for the collection of elastic bands, which he would carry round, one in each hand, and another hanging from his mouth. Attendance at school, whilst successfully banishing his fear of crowds, never enabled him to form a real friendship.

At times it seemed as if, in fact, he possessed a veritable treasure house of speech which he could use if he so chose. This, of course, is the romantic view of autistic children – but it still seems to me incomprehensible that, if sufficiently roused and involved, speech came veritably tumbling out. For instance, Simon loved accidents. They shone out in his life. If I dropped a dish in the kitchen, he would exclaim spontaneously, with high glee, "Mummy break dish. Naughty Mummy. Dish went crash. Poor dish." What is more, he did not say it once, but hundreds of times, reminding me of what I would have preferred to forget for days, even weeks afterwards. Nor was his interest confined to mishaps concerning objects – those occurring to people enchanted him even more. "Charlie fell, in the nettles," he told me, returning from school one day, a broad smile on his face. "Poor Charlie. Charlie cry." And day after day Charlie went on falling in the nettles until he achieved something of a legendary status in the eyes of the rest of the family. Sometimes I wonder if Simon's speech would have developed more if we had contrived an endless series of "accidents" to keep him feeling this imperious need to comment. Well, we were not brave enough to try, but I am left frequently wondering at the strangeness of this handicap which gives a child, as those outbursts proved, the mechanism of useful speech whilst omitting to allow him the fuel to power it, the embodiment of an energy crisis in an industrialized state.

However, in those earlier days that I am writing of here, this switching on and switching off phenomenon was not yet clearly visible, and I plugged on doggedly with the reading, keeping a diary that recorded all the daily "progress". I smile now at the optimism of that diary. Yet I don't smile bitterly, for without that optimism I could not have maintained my efforts, and in making those efforts I was building something which was of far greater value than the number of words mastered: a very real relationship with my withdrawn son. And at the same time, the wound in me was beginning to heal, for channelling thought and energy into this project gave me the satisfaction of knowing that I was doing my best to help. It gave Simon something, too – an experience that was vital to him – the realization that he could win praise and enjoy attention, the feeling of being a special person in someone else's eyes. I think that through "reading" Simon began to discover himself.

In terms of the skill of reading itself, the attempt still cannot be written off as an out and out failure. When, in later years, Simon went on to an ESN school, I was asked to give up reading with him at home so that the teachers might gain a clearer idea of the success of their own methods, and to avoid confusing the child. After a year or two, we were encouraged to take it up again, and I found that he had gained in fluency, and to some extent in comprehension. He never forgot anything he had once really learned.

Today, at home, he does not spontaneously pick up a book and read it for pleasure, by himself. To that extent we have failed. But it does give him great pleasure to be asked to read by someone else, with the same childish delight in praise that he showed as a small boy. Several years of highly sophisticated teaching have caused his comprehension to soar, so that he can now enjoy the experience far more, even if he cannot share in all the emotions expressed by the written words. He can follow simple television stories, though he shows a marked preference for slapstick comedy – accidents again, I think!

But whatever the ratio of success and failure, teaching

Simon to "read" stands out as a high spot in all my memories of his early years. For it brought me my first taste of honest delight in my handicapped son, and caused me to realize that delight was not only still possible, but that it was actually deeper and greater *because of* the handicap. It made other parents' pride in the brilliance of their normal children seem positively trivial. For us, the task, the difficulties, the responsibility were all so much greater – and so, correspondingly, was the reward. This was the first manifestation of the change in my scale of values. From now on, I was dealing with basics, and I had learned, the hard way, to distinguish them for what they were. I knew now how to look for, and find, delight in the smallest things. That, for me, was the most important discovery I ever made.

5

"If music be the food ..."

Now that I had discovered that there was a new kind of happiness to be found in working to help Simon, happiness both for him and for me, I began to wonder if there were not more that I could do, if there were not perhaps other ways of getting through to him that would reinforce the advance of the reading sessions. The success of these depended to a large extent on harnessing his extraordinary powers of memory. Was there any other area of natural ability that could be exploited so as to increase the amount of contact he was able to make with other people?

To me, one of the most mystifying aspects of autism is the undisputed fact that many autistic children do possess such areas of special ability, or "islets of intelligence" as the experts call them, whilst being retarded in every other way. Within these areas their mind appears to function not only normally, but even extra well. Usually, the skills involved are non-verbal. One autistic young man, for instance, succeeded in obtaining a degree in mathematics. Another, year after year, took the first prize for painting at the Royal Academy exhibition of art by handicapped children. A large number have an exceptional response to music – some have eventually found employment as piano tuners. Small wonder that the uninitiated parent, confronted with the eccentricities of the still undiagnosed autistic toddler, can be completely thrown by these strange manifestations of unusual skill – the four year old who counts up to a hundred and back, in threes, with perfect ease, or, as in our case, the two year old who sings, with perfect pitch and passable pseudo-French, a complicated French folk-song.

There was never any real doubt in my mind that Simon was anything but extremely musical. Once, I had let the obvious presence of some sort of musical talent blind me to everything else that was wrong. Now, I was seeing clearly again, and was better able to weigh the potential of what talent he had. I do not mean that I foresaw a possible future for him as a concert pianist, but I did begin to wonder if this special response to music might also be harnessed into working for him. Music, after all, is a means of communication, with the advantage that it communicates emotion. Simon, isolated from all but the most superficial emotions by his deprivation of language, could surely be reached, and helped to grow by means of music. But how?

I sat back and took stock of our assets. It stood to reason that if I wanted to use music in our daily life, I would have to be closely involved myself. The difficulty here was that I am only a very mediocre musician, although I have a very deep love of music. My two brothers and myself were all given piano lessons by our parents not because our parents were musical – they weren't – but because it was the nice thing to do for your children in those days, and did not cost too much. By the time it *did* cost too much, and my lessons stopped, I had gained enough technique to accompany enthusiastically, if inaccurately, provided that no one was feeling too ambitious and the accompaniment was not too exposed. I also loved singing, and managed, through church choirs and university choral societies, which did not cost anything at all, to acquire a modicum of musical knowledge. All of which had been great fun, but so much enthusiastic mediocrity did not look to be much of a qualification when it came to teaching a mentally handicapped child. I could have tried to teach him the rudiments of playing the piano, but even I had the wit to see that the piano, as an instrument, presented insurmountable difficulties for a child with poor physical coordination and a very limited attention span. But I did not have the least idea how to play anything else. It was war-time when I was at school, and there were absolutely none of the opportunities for learning musical instruments that exist for children now – at least, not in State schools. So that I had no real idea how to go about instructing Simon in the first steps of learning an instrument, even if I could manage to teach him to read musical notation.

All, it seemed, that I could do was to give him every possible opportunity of listening to music with me, and of singing with me. It was not enough, and I knew it, but though I asked every musical friend I knew, no one seemed to be able to suggest anything better.

Then another of our famous "coincidences" occurred. The same friend who had given me the article on reading, now discovered one in the same magazine – *Where* – on music therapy. I read it almost disbelievingly, so exactly did it answer all my questions, and reaffirm my own belief that music could indeed help the handicapped. There even existed, it seemed, a society based on this very principle. The article thoughtfully gave the name and address of the secretary, and I immediately sat down to write to her, and to tell her about Simon. She wrote back very promptly, inviting me to take him to see her.

A week or so later, we found ourselves in a quiet house in Highgate, in a room full of musical instruments, talking to a fragile, grey-haired lady with a lively face and compassionate eyes. At least, I talked to her – Simon had followed his usual practice of ensconcing himself behind a convenient cupboard door, and was opening and shutting it as if nothing else in the world existed.

This unsociable behaviour did not disconcert our new friend in the least. She merely took out a somewhat weird assortment of simple instruments, and told me that she was going to test Simon's reaction to sound. I watched, fascinated.

First, she merely tapped on a block of wood with a small drumstick. He did not appear to notice the tapping in the least. Then she beat on a small drum. He just went on opening and shutting his door. Undiscouraged, she shook a set of tinkly sleigh bells. Still no response. Then, smiling to herself, she set out a group of chime bars, and gently struck one of them with a flexible rubber hammer. As its lovely, rounded note swelled out into the room Simon froze – and then looked to see where the sound had come from.

Again she struck the note, whereupon he abandoned the safety of his cupboard door, hurried across the room, snatched the hammer from her, and played the note himself, an ecstatic smile on his face. It was the first time I had ever seen him voluntarily abandon an obsessive activity, and the significance of his action was not lost on me. It confirmed my hunch that if only he could be taught to build on this innate musicality, then here was another way in which he might, as it were, skirt his handicap – enter into communication with other people without using words. Miss Alvin's next action demonstrated the truth of this – she picked up another hammer, and softly played at the same time as Simon, using the notes of the pentatonic scale, so that the sounds were always harmonious.

"See," she said to me, "Simon and I are talking."

I was very close to crying.

After playing with Simon for a little while, to their mutual enjoyment, she left him to continue by himself, while she explained to me how I might become his music therapist, despite my obvious limitations. She emphasized that music should always be regarded as a learning activity, and that I should never let it deteriorate into a mere excuse to play around with the instrument, otherwise there was a risk that it, too, could just become another obsession. Her instructions were clear and simple, but I took notes, just in case. She also made it plain that I could refer back to her at any time when I felt I needed help. Before I left, rather as an afterthought, I asked her if, since Simon so much enjoyed listening to music, there were any particular works which could be of actual benefit to him. She recommended several, and I little thought, as I carefully wrote down Smetana's "Vltva" from "Ma Vlast", Dame Myra Hess playing "Jesu Joy of Man's Desiring", and Saint-Saëns "The Carnival of the Animals" – these were named as a starting point – just how well I was to grow to know them in the months to come, especially the Smetana, which enchanted Simon as he followed the transformation of the tiny mountain stream to the great river, with its crashing, thrilling descent over the waterfall. We wore that record right out.

I went home feeling both exhilarated and supported – supported as I had never felt until that day. Now, at last, we really had some guidance, and I knew what I was trying to do.

First of all, I had to acquire my chime bars. Even in those "never had it so good" days they were not cheap. Fortunately, a birthday was at hand, and friends and relatives were roped in to help. Once again I set to drawing flash cards, but this time with musical notes and staves on them. A raid on the rag bag brought forth several pieces of highly coloured cloth in which

Simon might wrap his chime bars separately. For he had to be taught to cherish his musical instrument, to treat each note, in fact, as if it were a person. From the first, he was put in charge of the unwrapping and re-wrapping of each chime bar at the beginning and end of each session. What is more he had to learn to greet each one individually as he brought it out, by name, and to say goodbye to it as he put it away. He needed very little persuasion to do this, and before long "Hello A" or "Hello C" became a matter of expected routine. Shortly after this, he began to greet actual people, too. His music therapy was beginning, even if only very slightly, to affect his everyday life.

He quickly learned to play several tunes, and would sing or hum as he played. But he learned more than this, for through his activities on the chime bars, the meaning of several words became clear to him. He loved to demonstrate his comprehension as I asked him to play fast or slow, loud or soft, up or down. Wrapping the notes as we did in their different cloths taught him the names of the different colours, so that he could pick out the red cloth or the green cloth upon request. I have often wondered if the colours did not come to have some association for him with the sound they enclosed, for each note was always wrapped in the same colour, and I deliberately chose warm, deep colours for the low notes, and paler ones as we ascended the scale.

Simon accepted the discipline of our music sessions well, and did not rebel against their very simple structure. As with the reading sessions, I kept their length very short, and I *did* remain firm over one point: they were exclusive to Simon. Joanna, however much she cajoled or stormed, was not allowed to be present. (This seems ironic now, when, at rising thirteen, it is clear that she is growing up into a very gifted 'cellist!) Miss Alvin had been adamant about this, however – Simon's instrument was to be his especial friend, and his alone. Sharing it would destroy all its value for him.

We continued working happily with the chime bars for several months. Then I noticed that his attention was beginning to wander, and his enthusiasm to diminish. He would still come and tug me by the hand after lunch, saying, "Time for music," but by the time he had played one tune, he had had enough. I was not sure what to do, so I got in touch with Miss

Alvin. She invited us along to see her again. Once there, she reassured me that this change in Simon was perfectly normal. It simply signified that he was ready to move on to a new stage. We would try him out with percussion – and the company of other children. She tested his reaction to percussion instruments, and found that although he did respond to drum beats, and would imitate them, he was far more enthusiastic about cymbals. He would clash them, then lift them up close to his ears, so that he might not miss a single vibration, again with an ecstatic smile on his face.

A bad time was beginning for our neighbours. Again, I sent out an SOS to the family for help in building up a good set of percussion instruments – cymbals, tambourines, triangles, tom-toms, castanets, sleigh-bells and maracas – and a lovely, deep bass drum.

I invited every child I could lay hands on to join our "band". Now at last Joanna, too, could join in, to her great excitement; and somewhat to her surprise our Dutch *au pair* found herself part of it. The din was unbelievable as they all joined in round the piano, with me at the keyboard belting out the tune in a way that would have startled my mother, who had only rarely succeeded in persuading me to practise. And here was Simon in the middle of it all, clashing his cymbals perfectly on the beat, loving every moment, and sharing his enjoyment with other children – a long way indeed from his cupboard doors.

Sadly, however, it was only a couple of months or so after the inauguration of these sessions that he began daily attendance at a new, experimental autistic unit some fifteen miles from our home. Much of his day (exactly how much I did not then suspect) was taken up in travelling, and he was very tired when he came home. It grew more and more difficult to fit in our percussion raves. They developed into a treat, reserved for wet weekends and holiday time.

I was unhappy about this, but there seemed very little that I could do about it. Education authorities did not share my views about the importance of music therapy for a musical autistic child, so there was no hope of finding a teacher who could teach him individually at school. I was expecting Tom by this time, and there was no longer either the time or the energy to make the long trip to see Miss Alvin. She did not know of any music therapist in our area who could take over from her. I asked every musician I knew, yet again, but all to no avail. I had, it seemed, started something I could not sustain, and it made me very sad.

For the next four years or so, we simply kept going as best we could, with singing, listening to music, and, occasionally, making up a band. It was very frustrating, like possessing the bulb of a rare lily, and being unable to watch it grow for lack of suitable nourishment. Something, however, was happening. During this fallow musical period, Simon's social behaviour was improving. He had been transferred from the autistic unit to an ESN school a little nearer our home, and here his tolerance of other people, and children in particular, made rapid strides.

Greatly daring, we decided to try taking him with us to operas and concerts. His first opera was Mozart's *Il Seraglio*. We had taken a box so that we might make a discreet exit if the need arose, but it never did. Simon behaved impeccably, better in fact than many of the "normal" adults around him. He was enthralled by the whole thing – the atmosphere of treat, the colours and bright lights, the orchestra conveniently placed just beneath us, and the marvellous singing.

We had borrowed the score from the local library, so that he could recognize several of the catchier tunes. Occasionally, I could hear him joining in with a low hum just beside me, but this was absolutely the only sound he made. After this first successful experiment, we took him to many operas, and were able to relax and enjoy ourselves as well, confident that he would not let the side down, while his smiles of delight amply re-paid any expenditure. I also found that the usually very formal opera audiences unbent considerably when Simon and Joanna accompanied us – I had never before actually experienced being *offered* chocolates by total strangers when attending some very grand performance. Simon's good looks, supported by his sister's charm, no doubt had something to do with this.

During these years, he was also maturing physically. His poor coordination, particularly noticeable when he was running, or clambering in and out of the car, was undoubtedly improving. Also, his comprehension of language, though it outdistanced by far his powers of spontaneous speech, had increased beyond hope. In fact, by the time I was at last successful in finding him a music teacher, when he was ten, Simon was far better equipped to cope with learning an instrument. The frustrating years of waiting had not been entirely wasted.

I had been galvanized into yet another round of writing to likely people by this same humming which I had first noticed at the opera. It was as if Simon was unable *not* to join in any music he particularly liked, so deep was his love of it. I used to find myself playing the piano with Simon standing at my elbow, humming the melody in my ear. If I played a wrong note, he stood there patiently humming the right one until I came to heel. My husband received the same treatment, so, too, did Joanna. They both put up with it remarkably well.

Miss Alvin had always insisted that Simon could not really differentiate between the music of different composers of the same period. Having watched him over the years, however, I would now venture to disagree, and Joanna would support me. He can always distinguish the music of Johann Sebastian Bach, and this is the music that he loves above all other. When I struggle to play one of the easier Partitas on the piano, he does not hum one single line of notes, but puts in, correctly, as many as it is humanly possible to do with one voice. His whole body responds to the beat, and he seems to revel in the intricacy of the counterpoint. "Play Bach," he says, with a deep sigh of pleasure, as the piece comes to an end, and frequently there is nothing for it but to play it through again. I have often wondered at this predilection, but can only surmise that it has something to do with the structured quality of the music, which gives him a feeling of security.

Eventually, my persistent search for a teacher was rewarded. It had to be – or so I felt – for so great a love as this could not be forever denied. I found my way to the office of the assistant county music adviser, and there, told her all about Simon and our long search for a local therapist and teacher. She listened with sympathy and interest, and, an hour later, we walked out with the name and phone number of a recorder teacher who would not only be willing to try to teach Simon, but who would actually come and do so in his own home. The assistant county music adviser came very near to being hugged. I could not believe this wonderful luck. Then I tried very hard to calm down. I had to wait and reserve my

judgment. The whole thing might well misfire. I had no idea
how Simon was going to respond to a stranger teaching him
music.

Neither had Valerie. She was, in fact, a little nervous when
she first came to see us and discuss the possibilities. She is a
teacher, not a music therapist, and she had never taught an
autistic child before. During the first three half-hour lessons,
they tested each other out – Simon bent on seeing how much
playing about he could get away with, and Valerie on discovering how much pressure she could bring to bear on him. By the
fourth lesson she had won him over to complete interest and
concentration for the whole half hour. He loved his lessons –
there was no doubt about that – I could tell by the way his
face lit up when I told him that Valerie was coming.

For some time she taught him almost exclusively by ear, so
that he should get to know his instrument in itself, as it were.
She gradually built up a repertoire of some twenty tunes, cunningly inserting rhythm exercises between them, and later
began to re-introduce him to musical notation. He seemed to
have forgotten very little of what he had learned with me in
those early sessions with the chime bars, and it was not long
before he was beginning to sight-read.

As she herself played with a very beautiful, liquid tone, he
naturally did his best to imitate her. In fact, he did his best for
her in every way, for he became very attached to her. One of
his greatest achievements was to hold his part valiantly
while she put in a harmony around it. He always used to smile
slightly as he did this, as if thinking what a lovely game this
was that he was playing with his teacher.

Since one of our declared aims was to enable Simon to play
with other people, I decided that I had better learn the
recorder as well. To tell the truth, I had been amazed that it
could ever sound as beautiful as it did when Valerie played it
– the first time I heard her, I had mistaken it for a flute. At
first I hitch-hiked on the back of Simon's lessons – Valerie
gave me five minutes all for myself at the end of Simon's
half hour. But as my interest grew, this simply was no longer
enough, and before long her visits began to last for an hour
– half for Simon, and half for me. In this roundabout way
began one of the most fascinating and absorbing hobbies I
have ever had – I could not wait to possess the whole family

of recorders – sopranino, descant, treble, tenor and bass, so that we might learn to play part music at home, in the family, making it for ourselves instead of always depending on others. And it is all thanks to Simon, and, of course, Valerie, who, before she gave up teaching, introduced me, my hands slippery with apprehension, to my first recorder consort.

For give up teaching she unfortunately had to do. As the time for the birth of her first baby grew nearer, playing the recorder became something of a physical impossibility, and the day came when, sadly, we had to say goodbye.

We were on our own again. For a while, I tried to keep up Valerie's work, but I lacked her experience, and musical imagination and facility. Besides, I now felt strongly that Simon was at an age when he should be taught by people other than his mother, if I was not to risk having all his interest and affection unhealthily centred on me. There was also a quite basic question of time. By now I had David to look after, as well as Tom, while Joanna's music demanded its fair share of my involvement. By the time Simon went away to boarding school, when he was twelve, we had, very sadly, lost a lot of ground.

I still feel frustrated that his potential in this field has never been fully developed. Circumstances, it seems, have always been against us. His own striking love of music, and the fact that Joanna and Tom are, barring accidents, both likely to become gifted musicians, indicate that Simon, had I only been able to come up with continuity of skilled teaching, might have achieved much more than he actually has. Now that he is away from home, the matter is largely out of my hands – I can only try to see that he joins us in some form of musical activity during his visits home.

What I really wanted for him was that he should be given the chance to attain a level of competence which would have enabled him to play in an amateur band or orchestra, so that he might enjoy this social experience on a regular basis. I do not think that I was crying for the moon, and I do believe that it would have given him a great deal of benefit and pleasure, as well as a means of emerging from his isolation.

As things turned out, we could not give Simon this gift chiefly because we do not live in the right place. Although there are plenty of musical activities in the area where we live, music therapy is not one of them, and there are very few music teachers who are prepared to try to teach a mentally handicapped child.

On the other hand, I feel sure now that we did give him something. Neither he, nor the other children will ever quite forget, I feel sure, even when they are grown up, our glorious percussion sessions, and the warmth and laughter they generated, however grey the world outside. Nor will any of the rest of us ever forget the smile on Simon's face when he joins in well known tunes during sing-songs round the piano. There is something robustly old-fashioned in the flavour of this family activity whereby we create our own pleasure – something handed down from times when families really were families, too numerous for expensive toys and treats, dependent therefore on home-grown talents and imagination. Since these can thrive despite material poverty, they can be a source of security.

This year I had the good old maternal thrill of seeing my son play in the school concert. Simon's boarding school, Somerset Court, gave a concert to help school funds, and put on a special show for parents. As I watched him standing there by himself, playing "Blow Away the Morning Dew" on his recorder, looking extremely pleased with himself, I reflected that it did not really matter in the least if he now played it at much the same level as he had four years ago, with Valerie. What mattered was the distance he had come since, as a child of four, he had first left the haven of Juliette Alvin's cupboard door to investigate the sound of the chime bars. Even if he had never completed his journey, he had come further than I would then have believed possible.

And yet ... I cannot help the sigh ... if only there were more music therapists ...

6

Pegasus

Simon was seven when we saw the picture in *The Times* that gave us so much food for thought: a mounted police officer helping his handicapped son to sit on a horse. We found it very moving, though there was nothing dramatic about it. Perhaps it was the expression of pride and pleasure on the faces of both father and son. A short feature accompanying the photo discussed how horse-riding could help the handicapped.

We kept the picture on display on the kitchen pin-board. We thought about it a lot, and we were both thinking the same thing: do you think that maybe Simon . . . ?

Already he had changed a great deal since the daemonic days immediately after the diagnosis, and was a great deal easier to live with. The screaming fits had almost completely disappeared – thanks largely, I suspect, to the discipline of school. He seemed to have acquired a working idea of what was expected of him by way of behaviour, and did his best to live up to it. He had very little spontaneous speech, but tried hard to answer questions and succeeded with the help of a little prompting. I always felt that he regarded this question and answer business as some sort of test devised by adults – if he managed to say what was required, he passed, but if not, he was failing us however much we encouraged him. I am certain that he never looked on the exchange of information as a rewarding pastime, much less as a pleasure, and does not to this day. Silence is so much easier, and safer.

He conformed so well, and still looked so normal that strangers rarely realized that he was handicapped until they tried to enter into conversation with him, or observed him with more than superficial interest. Only then did they realize the existence of the language barrier, and of my arch-enemy, the apathy, the total absence of a vital spark of interest that I had noticed in him in Alexandra's house, as a baby. Even now, despite our efforts with reading and with music, despite the training that he was receiving daily at school, he still seemed to be unable to initiate any purposeful activity. Someone always had to prod him. If no one did so, he would simply sit alone, twiddling his piece of broken plastic, his eyes blank, his mouth slack. It was the aloneness that hurt me for him. Other children came home from school and plunged into a whirl of activities, talking, playing, watching TV. Simon quite liked watching TV, but usually I was pretty sure that it was without comprehending what he saw – unless it happened to be pure slapstick comedy, or wrestling, which to him was much the same thing.

The passage of time was making it clear that he needed a whole range of activities to keep him awake and growing mentally. Reading and music were fine in their way, but they were not enough. Unfortunately all competitive sports were out, for the simple reason that they were competitive, and Simon still could not understand what winning meant. To develop him physically, therefore, we needed activities that were enjoyable in themselves, whether or not one excelled at them – walking, swimming, or – perhaps – riding.

He enjoyed going for walks, and we have the luck to live in a village surrounded by beautiful countryside, but we were hampered by the presence of toddlers, who shared neither the grown-ups' enthusiasm, nor their stamina. We tried swimming, and turned out on many an early Sunday morning at the local baths. In the short term this achieved more for Joanna, who as a result learned to swim before she was five, than it did for Simon. He was in two minds about the water. He obviously loved the feel and the taste of it, and enjoyed wading around in it, but he was also extremely nervous of losing his balance, and would not under any circumstances submit to being held or lifted. In fact, had we known it, we were laying down a very good foundation for future aquatic activities by simply resigning ourselves and letting him be, wading happily around and sucking the chlorine from his fingers. It took another six years before his confidence reached the point where he could be induced to take his feet off the bottom.

Thus it seemed that the photograph in *The Times* had appeared somewhat on cue. Perhaps riding might prove to be the activity he could enjoy, whilst opening up his horizons a little.

We hesitated a long time. All animals other than our placid, furry cats alarmed him. He was frightened by the unpredictability of their movements. We, too, were afraid of increasing this fear by putting any extra pressure on it. We did not want to do anything that might impede the general progress he was undeniably making. Nor did we want to push him beyond his capabilities. We had been told too often, and too pointedly, about parents of handicapped children who try to force their offspring into a kind of skill-gathering, so as to make them appear more normal, thereby lessening their own embarrassment, and perhaps guilt. We agreed that such forcing was wrong, and that it was done for the worst of reasons. But these, we knew, were not our reasons. We felt that the acquisition of the skill could be, in itself, the source of pleasure and satisfaction to a child, without taking it any further than that. The life of a mentally handicapped person, by now I was sure of this, is of necessity of a different quality from that of a normal person, but it does not *have* to be a life of total sensual and intellectual poverty. Whether or not our mentally handicapped children go through life empty-handed and empty-headed depends ultimately on us, their parents, their teachers and their friends, if they are lucky enough to have any. Their poverty is their dependency. By themselves, they can achieve nothing. Already our own experience had borne this out. And we had seen Simon grow a little, in his own eyes as well as in those of the rest of the family, with each new accomplishment, however small.

So, in the end, we decided to give horse-riding a try. I felt that if, at the very least, he could learn to enjoy the pleasures of rambles on horseback – on a leading-rein of course – this would add at least something to his constricted life. We had little hope that he would ever learn really to ride and control a horse. That seemed too much to ask of someone whose handicap consisted basically of the inability to communicate. But we thought that even if he could experience only a small part of the activity, we would be giving him something of very positive value.

It was with no little trepidation that I approached one of our local riding stables and explained our requirements to the manager. I was relieved by his readiness to accept Simon as a pupil. Too relieved. In my fear of being rejected, I did not assess the teaching facilities critically enough. At that stage, I was too grateful for any kindness to be finicking in my demands. Perhaps, also, I had too little faith in Simon's potential – I did not really believe that he could be taught anything much about riding.

There was a lot for him to face up to on those first visits. The stable yard was overflowing with precisely the kind of creatures that alarmed him most: excitable dogs, flappy ducks and bantams, pigs and, needless to say, swarms of children. He clung to me. He was scared – but he was also fascinated, and relaxed as I talked to him, explaining all the activity.

He was utterly amazed to find himself being hoisted onto a pony's back. He found he could survey everything in total safety from this extraordinary new eminence. As we moved carefully off in the direction of the fields, a tentative smile spread over his face. This new form of movement was fun. I walked beside him, ready to catch him if he slipped, and to reassure him in case of fright. It wasn't really necessary. He balanced perfectly, as if instinctively. The hovering smile broadened and deepened into a look of intense pleasure. I could see him registering and approving each new sensation. I began to relax.

It was tame indeed as rides go, but there was nothing tame about it in Simon's eyes. There was snow on the ground, and, as we picked our way through the cold woods, I saw him look around. His eyes were clear and focused. In my heart, I cheered. Simon had switched on. He was receiving the world.

This kind of riding went on for some months. I did not always accompany him. Occasionally I went down to the field to watch him performing simple exercises, or jolting round the track as a helper yanked the unwilling pony into a trot. I could see that he had no idea of what he was doing, or of the reason for doing it. He was being "taught" by a very young and unqualified girl, who, although she always seemed kind to him, had only the haziest notions of his particular difficulties, and who was too diffident and quiet herself to instil any confidence into him. Certainly, he was enjoying riding, but he was remaining completely passive. He was not making any effort. Suddenly, it dawned on me that this was not enough. Now that my initial fears had been exorcized, I suspected that he was capable of doing far more than I had ever dared hope, with rewards that would be correspondingly greater. I decided to try elsewhere.

We approached a different stable. Again, I explained the circumstances. Again, we were kindly received, and again, I still had not properly weighed up our requirements. This was a large, and extremely professional establishment. There were many instructors, all qualified, and all impeccably turned out. Hundreds of children from all over the area attended weekly for lessons – though we never saw another one there like Simon. Teaching in these stables was efficient and thorough, and absolutely fine for any normal, well-adjusted child. But it was not right for us.

Not that Simon did not learn anything. He did, but learning was not for him the source of pleasure that I had grown to recognize as the only effective way of teaching him. The chief reason was that he had a series of different teachers, which meant that he could not possibly form a working relationship with any of them. They were all too busy to take time to get to know him outside the lesson, or to ask me about autism, so that none of them ever realized that he could not understand half their commands, filled as they were with, to him, incomprehensible prepositions and adverbs. He gained experience, however, and familiarity with the feel of a horse's back. He walked, he trotted, he cantered, he even fell off a number of different animals. He became accustomed to moving at different speeds on horseback, and the routines of mounting and dismounting no longer presented too much difficulty for him, beyond the fact that he always stuck halfway, which he found a bit of a joke. But he was still not really giving anything. Trotting remained a passive, bone-shaking experience, cantering was fun, provided that someone was close by, at the other end of a short leading rein, to haul the pony along. He had no more idea that he might communicate with the animal than he had of entertaining any special feeling for his teachers.

It is interesting, looking back on this time, to see how the whole project grew and took shape. We had started out expecting nothing more than a certain amount of extra pleasure for Simon. Then, very much as had happened once we found our way to a music therapist, we discovered that the pleasure could lead to learning and growing, so that unconsciously we began to expect far more, both of him and of his teachers.

In the end we realized that the place, good as it was, was bad for Simon. It was, quite simply, too big, too busy, and too impersonal for him. Reluctantly, and with increasing misgivings about ever finding a place that could really help him, we decided to try one more move – to a third stable, a couple of miles from our home. The moment we set foot in it, and watched Simon having his first lesson, we knew that we had found what we wanted. There was something in its atmosphere that had been lacking from the other two – a kind of warmth. The stable belonged to a large family who lived in a neat house beside the yard, and the warmth, I found, stemmed from them.

The family feeling extended to the thirty-odd ponies who lived and worked there. Each one was cared for and loved as an individual. The yard was spotlessly clean and bright with fresh paint, the animals were smartly turned out, but there the smartness ended. The family atmosphere attracted other families, whole clans of them, and not all could afford more than the bare essentials of riding gear. It didn't seem to matter. Everyone was friendly. Within a couple of weeks they all seemed to know Simon, and welcomed him warmly – he had become one of the family.

At that time, classes were run by the youngest daughter. I only had to watch Sue working with Simon once to realize that we had stumbled upon not only the right, but the ideal teacher for him: young, pretty, strong of voice and character and, above all, overflowing with warmth and compassion. She was, I saw, the pivot of the whole place: children loved her, and respected her fluent commands, the ponies trusted and obeyed her. I have never forgotten the commotion which reigned one evening round a pony that had fallen in its box and could not get up. It was becoming wild with fear, and was in danger of twisting its gut in its efforts to rise. Nobody seemed able to quieten it until Sue arrived on the scene. Taking no notice of the desperately flailing hooves, she entered the box, knelt down, took the pony's head in her lap and talked to it, crooned to it as if it were a baby, and continued until the eyes had stopped rolling and it lay quiet, while the others quickly stacked straw around it to help it regain a grip on the floor. It trusted her absolutely. Small wonder the other assistants liked and listened to her. And Simon? In Simon's case it was the first *coup de foudre* of his life. He would have ridden the Grand National if she had been there to shout him on. We had only been to the stable a few times, when, telling him we were going riding, I asked him who we were going to see. "See Sue!" he replied, with a note of distinct determination in his voice.

To my complete amazement and near-incredulity, Sue had Simon rising to the trot within six weeks of starting to teach him. Then she had him sitting to it. Then she had him doing either, on command. She did not often take him out on hacks, where his attention would be too easily distracted – unless she felt that for some reason he was less likely to respond to instruction that day and needed variety – but kept him in the corral, and worked him on the lungeing rein.

He responded to her voice in a way I have seen him respond to few other people. It was a deep, strong, gravelly voice, unusual in a woman, with an instinctive authority of its own – perhaps that is what got through to him. He seemed to understand her commands when he appeared not even to hear those of another person. Sue's riding lessons galvanized him. My romantic visions of quiet rambles on horseback through woods and fields had undergone a complete transformation. Riding a pony was helping him far more than I had ever dreamed possible.

After each lesson, which I was always welcome to watch, we discussed the progress made, and the difficulties we were likely to encounter in the next stage to be attempted. Sue was never too proud or busy to ask me about aspects of Simon's behaviour which she did not understand. She quickly learned to substitute pictorial words for the usual riding-school words of command. "Raise both arms" became "Be an aeroplane", for instance, or "Squeeze with your heels", reduced to a far more graphic "Tap-tap-tap on Dolly's side". The difficulties of teaching so physical an activity to a non-verbal child were obviously manifold, but I never saw Sue despondent, or devoid of a suggestion for overcoming them.

Above all, she tried to encourage Simon to recognize the ponies he rode as individuals who could understand and respond to what he had to tell them. He needed quite a lot of persuading to hold a pony by its bridle – I think he found it quite a shock to discover that there was more to the animal than just a nice, high, safe back, but that it had eyes, an inquisitive nose, and teeth as well! But Sue insisted that he say "Thank you" after each ride, with a pat, and a piece of apple or a polo mint which was all too frequently dropped in a last moment panic as the great yellow teeth were bared to receive it. He never did quite lose his nervousness at this procedure, but if Sue asked him to do it, do it he would, and in the end he could be trusted to lead the pony back to its stall after his lesson.

Sue believed in Simon, and she believed she could teach him. That, I think was the secret of the whole story. I never once saw her at a loss, or resorting to sharpness of voice or manner when one of her ideas didn't work out. She rewarded every success, however slight, with warm praise, so that he always finished up in a glow of achievement, triumphantly echoing her "Well done, Simon" as he trotted back to the yard.

"Rise to the trot!" – he rose. "Sit to the trot!" – miraculously, his rump glued itself to the saddle. "Push her on, Simon, push Dolly on! Tap, Tap, Tap with your heels! That's right, *hard*er now – *splend*id!" – and his heels would give Dolly the faintest of nudges, to which she instantly responded, thanks to a discreet flick from Sue's long whip. "Now, shorten your reins" (she had demonstrated this to him many times until he understood) "hold on to the saddle, we're going to canter. Come on Dolly, *canter*!" Dolly would obligingly belt round at the end of the lungeing rein, encouraged by whip, Sue's fluent tongue, and, occasionally, a timid pressure from Simon's heels. He was one huge smile, he adored cantering. "Come on, Dolly, *canter*!" he would bellow, if she showed signs of flagging. Maybe he *was* just echoing Sue, but it certainly was a meaningful echo.

Dolly was not the most placid of ponies, although, like

all those in the stable, she was well schooled. I do not believe she had any mystical rapport with Simon, as is claimed by some authorities who maintain that horses develop a special feeling for handicapped riders. She behaved with him exactly as she did with all the other children who rode her. If he was supposed to be guiding her on his own, and did not show enough authority to halt her, she would take him ruthlessly back to her stall and ignore him. During trotting, she not infrequently checked, and sidestepped in a way that would bring many an inexperienced rider thudding to the ground. If Simon stayed on, it was due to his extraordinary gift of balance, not to Dolly's forbearance. In short, she made no special concession to her rider's difficulties. If she made any effort at all, it was in trying to provoke him into overcoming them.

I have seen Simon, when she had decided to try him out by taking time off for a snack of grass, thus jerking him forward in the saddle, tug her head up again, and shout, unprompted, "Not to eat grass! Naughty Dolly!" Sue and I looked at each other that day, and it was hard not to get tearful. The action, and above all, the command, showed us how far he had come. It was difficult for me to believe that this was the same child who had ambled through the snowy woods, two years previously, carried by an indolent pony, passive as a sack of potatoes. There was nothing indolent about Dolly, and nothing passive about her rider. This child was trying, and working, and learning.

It was that same year that Simon rose to what may well prove to be the summit of his career as a rider. The family who owned the stables wanted to build an indoor riding-school on their land, and had been refused planning permission as the land forms part of the Green Belt. (The fact that a six-lane motorway was to be built five years later a mere two hundred yards from their gates was conveniently overlooked.) They were resentful, feeling that the refusal was unjust, the more so because an indoor manège would have enabled them, as members of the Riding for the Disabled Association, to continue their weekly afternoon classes for children from a nearby centre for spastics despite the bad conditions in winter which frequently caused the cancellation of the classes and the disappointment of the children. Indignation ran so high that

they decided to stage a peaceful demo, on horseback, to hand
in a petition to the Prime Minister at 10 Downing Street. We
decided that the appeal would be even more effective if it were
handed in by one of the handicapped children who would
profit from the indoor school, and Simon, with his poignant
good looks, and newly acquired skills of horsemanship, was
the obvious candidate. The day that Simon rode Mole, Sue's
own old pony, down Whitehall at the head of a file of riders,
and, escorted by friends, politely handed in the petition at the
door of 10 Downing Street, seems something of a dream now,
but he did do it, and, what's more, he enjoyed doing it. He
did not seem in the least nervous. Of course, he did not understand the full import of what he was doing, but he seemed to
know that he was helping Sue. If he had understood, I am sure
that he would have done it just the same.

Finding a gifted, natural teacher is obviously a matter of
luck, or providence. Few people are endowed with the qualities
or skill, enthusiasm, authority and compassion mixed in the
right proportions. We found one of the few. On the other hand
we did push our luck and take a few risks. And the result
was worth every moment of fear and hesitation. The search
also taught us something, in that we had learned to recognize
the kind of teacher who could educate, in the full sense of the
word, our child. There was less chance of repeating our
initial mistakes in other fields.

These had occurred because perfectly good and qualified
teachers, not realizing the complexity of the autistic handicap, had not appreciated how important it was to consult with
us first. We, without understanding everything about autism,
were still through experience and observation, far more aware
of the difficulties of teaching him than they were. Misled, just
as we had been initially, by that beautiful, pensive, intelligent face, they made the huge mistake of assuming that
Simon could do all that other boys of his age could do "if
only he would wake up a bit". The trap was all the more cunningly hidden, in that, for example, the first two steps towards
horsemanship – climbing and balancing – Simon could ac-
complish with comparatively little difficulty, as could most
autistic children. All the rest presented a mountainous range
of difficulties owing to the problems of communication that
were involved – not just from the teacher to Simon, but also

from Simon to the pony. They did not know that – and they did not know simply because they did not ask us. Half the words which formed their commands were meaningless to Simon. As Sue was to discover, the "empty" words could be replaced by other, more graphic ones, but first one had to observe what he was and what he wasn't understanding.

"Come on, Simon, shorten your reins – you ought to know that by now." This impatient remark from Simon's first teacher was reported back to me by an indignant Joanna. "I don't think that was very kind, do you, Mummy? After all, he *is* handicapped." Joanna, at seven, already saw things and people very clearly. She already knew, as we did, and as Sue did instinctively, that you cannot say "ought to know" to an autistic child. There can be no "oughts" in the progress of someone whose handicap has no known cause, and no known cure. Each small step forward can only be achieved, if indeed it is to be achieved at all, by patient experiment combined with experience and love.

Sue provided all that. What is more, she was aware of the tremendous efforts Simon made to please her, how very, very hard he tried to follow her. "He really worked today," she said proudly, as she watched him dismount back in the yard, gently encouraging him to give Dolly the usual nervous "thank you" pat.

He began to draw horses soon after that, perfectly recognizable horses, with himself in the saddle, complete with hard hat. One day, he drew Sue as well, with huge authoritative hands. He really could not have paid her a greater compliment.

Eventually, our winning combination was once again broken up by circumstances: Sue left home and job to get married – though not before she had given Simon a chance to try his hand at jumping, to his entire delight. Once she had gone, however, nothing seemed the same. No one else, however much they tried, was ever quite able to replace her. Although Simon could not comment on her absence, it was obvious that he was looking for her, and mourned her departure. For a while longer we managed to keep up the riding, but as a family activity it was fated. For one thing, it was fast becoming very expensive, and, though we were given a special cheap rate for Simon, it seemed extremely cruel to Joanna, who was passionately addicted to the sport, to oblige her to accompany me to the stable to watch while Simon had his lesson. Problems were growing thick around us at that time.

So that door gradually shut. But soon after it had done so, as has so often been the case throughout Simon's life, another one opened. He went away to boarding school, and once more riding became available to him – as a school activity. He can't tell me much about it, so I don't know whether he still rises to the trot, and canters, and kicks his pony on – he just answers "yes" to all my questions. But I do know that he rides on the wide sands beside the Bristol Channel. I have been there, and it is beautiful. And I know from his smile that riding is something he delights to do. He can never quite lose the gift that Sue gave him – the experience of being in real contact with the back and brain of a living, responding, swiftly running horse. It is an experience which can enrich all human beings. For the Simons of this world – the deprived, the lame, the mentally handicapped – the horse can bear them for a while outside the confines of their restricted lives. And that is a gift without price.

7

"Home is where one starts from"

Although I have written about it in some detail in the fore-
going chapters, the teaching of Simon which we undertook
ourselves, or promoted elsewhere, was never allowed to grow
out of proportion, to dominate our family life. Soon after his
diagnosis, I had read a book entitled *The Birth of Language*
by Shulamith Kastein and Barbara Trace. In it the mother of
a non-verbal child describes in considerable detail the hours
and hours of intensive teaching she imposed upon her handicapped child, with the help of professional advisers. She
achieved a remarkable degree of success, and one cannot help
but admire her perseverance and determination, but in the
book she tends to gloss suspiciously lightly over the deprivation
this entailed for her two normal sons. At the end she goes to
some pains to assure us of their emotional balance and happiness, and this darkens my suspicions still further, for it is simply
not logical that such a degree of parental neglect should leave
no mark behind it. I came to the conclusion that such intensive
concentration on the handicapped child to the exclusion of the
others was an error of judgment. I did not want to make it if
I could possibly avoid it.

We consciously went on trying, as the family grew in size and
years, to incorporate what special attention Simon needed into
ordinary, everyday family life. In a way, the result is ironic.
The pleasure trying to teach Simon to read gave to us led
directly to teaching the other, younger children to do so as soon
as they displayed the least interest; so that out of the other
three, two were reading fluently by the time they started school,
and the third with only slight hesitation. Music therapy, as I

79

have described, affected the whole family, myself included. But when I first began to work at it with Simon, I had absolutely no idea that the other children were to prove in two cases extremely gifted, and in the third to have well above average response. It is quite true that Joanna, Tom and David started music lessons as soon as they could read words, but this was not because I had the slightest idea of any future talent. It was simply due to a theory I entertained – and still do – that one's enjoyment of music is greatly enhanced if one learns to read it at much the same time as learning to read books, so that both acts come equally naturally later in life. Nor could I have had, at that time, the remotest suspicion of the major role music, as a learning activity, was to play in helping us survive the second great crisis which befell us in later years, and of which I did not so much as dream in those days. Yet all our music making, and all the stimulus, originated with Simon's needs and Simon's pleasure.

Horse-riding, in fact, remained the only activity to be strictly Simon's preserve. This is really only because it is too expensive an activity for a large family such as ours. For a while Joanna was able to enjoy it too, and was in danger of becoming a conventionally horsy small girl, but in the end our private economic crisis forced her to give it up, admitting Simon's claim to priority with as good a grace as is possible in a twelve year old. Even so, riding had its effect on her in that it has left her with a deep love of all animals – to the point when our vet remarked on her fearless, yet gentle handling of our injured cat.

Obviously, in both reading and music, the three normal children soon outstripped the abilities of their handicapped big brother. To nip any feelings of superiority in the bud, I took pains to explain to each, as simply as possible, just why they were able to do this, and pointed out how exceptionally well-placed they were to use their skill to help him. I have often marvelled at the patience these otherwise ordinarily impatient children show with their big, slow sibling, and at the alacrity of their response to my requests for tolerance and understanding of his difficulties. They are no angels – I have no wish to play the fond mother – there have been plenty of occasions when they have forgotten to make concessions, or have simply found it easier to leave him out of their games, but it has rarely taken more than the gentlest of reminders from me to set them exercising their powers of invention so that a complicated game might include Simon, even if only in an ornamental role. I never really know to what extent Simon is aware of being left out of activities, and to what extent he suffers from such exclusion, since his features do not register a wide range of shades of emotion, but even a stranger could see his pleasure at being included, since it shines out of his face in a great smile. Later, once the novelty has worn off, this may well give way to a look of vacant boredom, until in the end he walks casually off to some obsessive activity of his own, leaving game and players callously in the lurch. This inability to become involved, coupled with his joy at being included, has been one of the principle obstacles to his full integration into family life. For a long time it worried me, until I began to realize that I was, once again, expecting too much, and that it was better to let things settle down into their own pattern of compromise, since when we have all felt ourselves under less of a strain.

The need for patience has not always been confined to Joanna, Tom and David – Simon, too, has been called upon to display it, and circumstances have forced me to be fairly ruthless about this. Since I am nervous of leaving him at home on his own, he has often been forced to sit through the other children's piano or 'cello lessons, or to attend what must have been for him very boring concerts and music competitions. He cannot share his brothers' and sister's passion for judo, so that many a club evening he has spent sitting with me at the edge of the mat, yawning widely, or occasionally smiling a tolerant, and faintly incredulous smile at his sister's antics. He never, ever protested, but would sit patiently on, enduring the incomprehensibility of the world for the sake of being at least physically with us. It was, I knew, a far from perfect state of affairs, but I could not think how to contrive anything better, and no one else offered any advice. In fact, I think it was probably right that both sides had to give, as well as to take.

Remembering those early days of conscious effort to teach Simon, and through the teaching to help him become an active member of the family, I think now that they were absolutely vital to my own recovery from the blow of the diagnosis, and the stress of the long years of worry. Through keeping my expectations low, I achieved most of them, which meant much to me though it may have appeared little to an outsider. Nowadays I strongly believe that acceptance of a handicap in one's child, one's friend, or for that matter oneself, must be active and positive, otherwise it cannot qualify for the definition. To sigh, murmur about the will of Allah, bow one's head and plod on, is not, as I see it, acceptance – it is merely fatalistic resignation, and it does not give much moral support. Accepting a handicap, physical or mental, surely means recognizing the existence of certain limits to one's activity, but refusing to regard them as definitive to the whole personality. It means consciously, continuously seeking to push them back by enriching all that is within them: it is the deaf Beethoven composing his choral symphony, the crippled Gauguin forcing out his colours, the spastic Joey writing his book with the help of his friends. Simon is no Beethoven, and he may never have the perceptions of a Joey, but he has certain precious human qualities which it would be criminal to neglect.

Once, after the false state of trundling him round the clinics, I had made the discovery that the action, if there was ever to be any action, had to begin at home, between our own two selves, the therapy, both Simon's and mine, was under way. It seems obvious now, though it wasn't then, that the beginning could only be at home, since that was the foundation of everything else.

Many might argue, reading this, that I had exceptional advantages, which are not the lot of all parents of handicapped children. It is true that there were several: we were affluent enough to afford help in the house, a car and the record number of driving lessons it took to teach me, by then no pliant teenager, to drive it. Above all, I had had a long and sophisticated education to give me confidence in all the necessary dealings with professionals.

When it came to the actual practice of teaching Simon, however, I am not sure that these advantages are really worthy of the name. Help in the house, in the shape of a succession of *au pairs* can quite often prove an added stress. Teenage girls, alone in a foreign country, are usually not without problems of their own, and who better to deal with them than the hostess, the surrogate mother. I still wince at the memory of the one who aborted a two and a half month pregnancy in my home while I was out, when I was six months pregnant myself. Certainly, the increased mobility granted by a car is an enormous help but even that can have its other side: if one has a car one is expected to do far more in terms of travelling, regardless of cost or the strain of long solo drives – so that I sometimes find myself taking on more than I can reasonably manage. And as for education – clearly it would be hypocritical to deny its personal value, but as an advantage when dealing with professionals such as psychiatrists or teachers, it has its drawbacks. Leo Kanner, when he first defined autism as a separate syndrome, noted that the parents of his group of autistic children were both highly educated *and* cold and aloof, and inferred from this a connection between education and lack of emotional warmth, without allowing for the effects of misery and bewilderment on a sophisticated mind. Teachers tend to be on the defensive, ready to take umbrage at the slightest suspicion of patronage or arrogance, even when not a shadow of either is present, which makes the relationship more than usually delicate.

No – I do not think that any of these so-called advantages were essential to making that first step towards real relationship with our autistic child. The truly essential ones lie in one's own personality as a parent, and as they are for the most part derived from one's own childhood experiences, warmed or chilled as they were by the presence or lack of affection, it would be somewhat hard to be held altogether accountable for them. The ability to love and constantly to demonstrate one's love, patience, and a dogged form of determination which refuses to be put off by the pessimistic utterances of the world – these are gifts, not to be self-made, and they can be found anywhere up and down the so-called social and educational scales. Such gifts can forge a means to help that child through teaching, whether it be to make pastry, saw logs, or to channel more complicated abilities in a profitable direction.

There is, however, also a natural disadvantage from which most of us suffer, and which, if one is not aware of it, can stifle the gifts, hampering their activities – and that is pride. One of the most unpalatable realities that you have to accept if you are the parent of a mentally handicapped child is that not only do you need help, but that you have to keep asking for it. It is not that other people do not want to help, but rather that they do not always know how to go about offering it without giving offence. Pride, the refusal to ask for needed help, can isolate the family far more than the handicap itself, for pride is like a shell, at once a refuge and an armour for the wounded and the vulnerable. You cannot communicate with a shell, for it is dead tissue, so that it effectively paralyses the growth of relationships with those around who might be sources of support. Nor is it likely to stimulate any contact with the child, who must find it hard to respond to the fixed self-image that is pride.

I was not exactly free of it, and I had to learn the hard way, through experience, how to break out of it. I discovered that sometimes I had to pester busy people to obtain what I wanted for Simon, and I shrank from doing it, as indeed I still do. Even a sensitive skin, however, will thicken with constant wear, and after a while mine, too, began to harden until I no longer minded if my name became mud in some quarters. Once the relationship with Simon began to grow, I was encouraged enough to make future requests for help far more confident, for they were based on purposefulness rather than self-pity.

Self-pity is inevitable, I think, for a time. Few outsiders realize the terrible deprivation of the parent of an autistic child, whose physical beauty makes the whole situation the more cruel. Normal human communication depends upon speech or a substitute for speech. To be the parent of an untrained autistic child means having a permanent, invisible barrier between you and the child which allows no such communication, no exchange of affection. You, the parent, have no idea of your child's thoughts – you don't really know whether he has any thoughts – and the child, it seems is unaware of yours. They can never, even when grown up, however tenderly you may have cared for them, give you any ordinary human comfort, however great your pain. They may even laugh at your tears, though not, of course, with malice.

The act of teaching can help you rise above all this. Teaching, however simple the level, is a form of giving which involves skill and, above all, self-control. In order to teach a child successfully, a certain objectivity is necessary, and it is this which can be so therapeutic to the parent, for it cannot co-exist with self-pity. Once you quit the role, if only temporarily, of hurt and frustrated parent to assume that of a teacher, the situation is transformed. The teacher has to put the child first, in order to observe the patterns of behaviour, to assess the possibilities of development and the obstacles that are or are not avoidable. The parent, as a teacher, re-discovers the child as an independent human being.

Of course it is infinitely better if the parent can do this under constant, regular, professional supervision, so that support can be given and crass mistakes avoided. In an ideal world such support would be available from the moment of diagnosis, indeed, not only available, but offered. In this real world of 1977, I have never yet met a single parent who has known it. It is perhaps inevitable, therefore, that I made at least one pretty crass mistake.

Certainly the one which scarred me, if not Simon, most was my failure to realize in time that just as my praise stimulated and inspired Simon to make great efforts to please me and so win more, the reverse was also true: my anger or even disapproval plunged him into misery. Without my knowing it, he had come to associate praise with love. Disapproval, therefore, meant for him the cessation of love. On the whole I succeeded in controlling irritability or impatience with him to a large extent (the others probably received more than their fair share as a result!), but on one occasion when I did lose this precarious control, I was brought up short by the realization of the kind of dependence I had created.

This was on the already mentioned occasion of the "apple clock", when he was about eight years old. I had gone into the sitting room and caught him red-handed in the act of stuffing the insides of our pretty carriage clock with chewed apple. I was alarmed out of all proportion to the act, for this was the first time I had known him do anything deliberately destructive entirely off his own bat – Joanna was usually the instigator of all misdeeds. I was very afraid that this new and unusual departure marked the start of a thoroughly anti-social obsession, which could soon reduce our home to tatters, and our friendships to remnants. The fear led me to express my disapproval far more strongly than was customary in any of my dealings with Simon: I smacked him.

The result frightened me far more than the deed which had provoked the slap. He began to sob, to weep, and then to scream, but in a heartbroken, rather than obsessive way. I very seldom smacked any of the children when they were small, regarding physical punishment as very much the last line of parental defence, and I probably had not smacked Simon for some considerable time, as he never did anything to merit desperate measures. Right then I felt far from happy about it. The violence of his reaction – violence such as I had not seen in his behaviour for a long time – made me feel that I had let him down, betrayed the intimacy of our new relationship. When, some two hours later, he was still sobbing and screaming as violently as ever, his whole face swollen, the skin around his eyes flecked with red, I felt as if I had committed murder. Nothing I could say or do would comfort or reassure him. Nothing in the world, nobody in the world could reach him in his abandonment and his misery. He was utterly alone. Eventually he exhausted himself, and, eight year old though he was, I put him to bed, where he at once fell deeply asleep. It was the kindest thing I could do: only a spell of unconsciousness could blur the edges of my betrayal. When he woke again, he was calm, but he would not look at me for the rest of the day, and the red flecks around his eyes did not fade away for a week. Needless to say, that was the last time I ever smacked him, and it made me apprehensive of even raising my voice. Reprobation, let alone punishment, was not something to be undertaken lightly with a child as vulnerable as this.

Even discounting this kind of mistake, I was no great shakes as a teacher. I could not continuously live up to my own ideals. There were days when enthusiasm was the last thing I could exude, when I wished the Ladybird readers and their inmates at the Antipodes, and the chime bars in outer space – days when we seemed to be making no headway whatsoever, and Simon seemed more, not less remote and incomprehensible. I was living among the trees and could not see the wood, as I can now. Today it is possible to understand how little those troughs mattered in the pattern of overall development, how, in fact, they are a necessary part of the teaching situation. It was my other children who taught me this. An excellent 'cello practice on Joanna's part is seldom, in fact never, followed by a second excellent one the subsequent day. Usually it is succeeded by a bad one, or at the most by an indifferent one, as if she needed to relax brain and muscles by standing still before taking off for the next jump. And the next jump always comes, in her own good time.

So, too, with the development of Simon's reading skill. (I took notes during the time that I worked most closely with him.) A spell of progress would be followed by a period of standing still, as it were, with an all but complete cessation of interest. That, in its turn would be followed by a distinct retrogression, when he appeared to have forgotten much that he had recently learned. Sometimes I would give up during these times and put the books away. Then, on bringing them out again after such a rest, it would be to find that he was in the middle of a new surge forward and had forgotten nothing. Until I was in a position to perceive a pattern, this was all most bewildering. It is easy to see the hazards of an unsupported one-to-one teacher-pupil situation.

Despite these hazards – my shortcomings, the incomprehensibility of Simon's handicap, the demands of the other children – I am aware now that I could not possibly have enjoyed the growing strength of our relationship had it not been for these attempts at teaching Simon. With more help from outside, they would probably have been far more successful in terms of practical results, but as it was, they were of enormous value to us emotionally.

There were also rewards which were totally unexpected. Whole new fields of interest opened up to me. I had, for instance, never suspected the existence of music therapy until I read the article in *Where*. Listening to Juliette Alvin experimenting with Simon's reactions to musical sound awakened a curiosity in me which is forever increasing. Why had the solid, round note of the chime bars penetrated his obsession when the lighter tinkle of the sleigh bells had not? I felt that in the answer, which I still do not possess, lie many fascinating clues to the riddles of human response to music. I still do not know why he so passionately loves the music of J. S. Bach, when that of other composers of the same period fails to stir him. I still do not know, but I promise myself a fascinating time studying to find out. The same applied to his, and other autistic children's love of motion – be it on a swing, a trampoline, or, as in Simon's case, on a cantering horse. (The same love of fast motion made teaching him to ride a bike a relatively easy process, despite his outrage when he fell off.) Speed, even at this relatively simple level of thinking and feeling, obviously has an enormous attraction. There can clearly be nothing meta-

physical about this – Simon is no Daedalus, he has no acquaintance with the gods. Again, I want to know more, for the
answer must contain some very basic facts about human
nature.

But perhaps the greatest reward of all, brought about by
growing contact with him, was the reformation, the crystal-
lization of my whole hitherto somewhat vague attitude to
education. The process of my own education had been successful in that it had channelled me to university and to a
degree, so that I had never questioned too deeply the merits
or de-merits of the path I followed. Hitherto we had not been
much concerned with the different systems as they affected all
children: only the academically bright merited our interest.
Simon changed all that. Because of him, I was obliged to dis-
card all conventional notions of success and failure, however
much these had governed my own career, and, in throwing
them out of the window in his case, I found that I was doing
it in the case of Joanna, Tom and David as well, for which
I think they may well have cause to be eternally grateful! Simon
taught us all the futility of running to keep up, and the value
of running for the sheer pleasure of it. It proved to be an invaluable lesson, and one which eventually helped us to survive.

Thanks then to this clumsy self-therapy, with its failures, its
struggles, and its rewards, Simon and I became more aware of
each other. Because of his enforced absence at work, my
husband was not able to join in very much, but he did what
he could when he could, reading with Simon when he came
home in the evenings, ferrying him to riding lessons at weekends, listening to and encouraging the music. He gave me as
much support as he possibly could, despite a very demanding
job.

What I had not altogether foreseen, and this because I had
so resolutely refused to look ahead, was that this kind of
therapy could only be transitory. As the problem of his official
education was gradually sorted out, though not without blood,
sweat, toil and tears, and he eventually began to attend school
full time, I had to accept that I must, for the most part, relinquish to others the job that I had so much enjoyed doing
myself. Most mothers experience this feeling when their children start school, but the experience is intensified with an
autistic child. I had real faith in only a very few teachers, for

I was all too aware that, through reading and my own daily experience I knew far more about autistic children than a teacher who had been trained only in a general way to teach mentally handicapped or retarded children. Even in those early days, I knew that the methods of teaching, say, a mongoloid child and an autistic child are not, or should not be, the same. The needs are different. I also knew that it did not behove me, a mere parent, a lay-man, to reveal this awareness and this knowledge.

I wanted Simon to go to school, obviously, but I wanted him to go to the right school, where his learning difficulties would be thoroughly understood. The fact that such a school was not immediately available made it far more difficult than usual to relinquish him to a stranger's care. However, I knew it was necessary, for both of us, and especially for him. His first steps away from the family and my apron strings had to be taken for both our sakes, but more particularly for his. Like any other child, he had to face the task of building relationships outside the home. But I was very frightened for him, frightened by his total innocence and vulnerability. He had absolutely no instinct whatsoever for self-defence, and yet he had to walk the ways of the world carrying this jewel of his outstanding physical beauty. I don't, upon very mature reflection, think it is all that surprising that I lived in a state of anxiety.

To my knowledge, nothing and nobody ever hurt him, and the time spent worrying was wasted. Now that he is nearly six feet tall I can relax a little, for I feel his size lends him a certain protection, even though it is only camouflage, for he is as gentle and docile as ever.

When Simon went off to school, I had to change roles again. I was, in fact, asked to stop working with him so that the school might assess its own methods. It was very hard to do this. I could no longer turn to the music therapy as, with a new baby and the fixed hours of Simon's long school day, there was no longer time to make the long journey to see the therapist. Perhaps it was this enforced inactivity which really fired the incentive to start the riding project. The school made no objections to this, nor, for that matter, did it show very much interest. This was a pity, as riding might well have benefited some of the other children. For us, it meant that we could still be closely involved in a learning activity with Simon. That was evidently what we needed, and I think it was important to him too.

The relationship we had built with Simon survived his going to school. It has so far survived his going to boarding school, though it is beset with new problems, to which I see no easy solution.

I am resigned to the fact that I will never know how much, if anything, I actually taught Simon, but one thing is vividly clear: I shall probably be learning to the end of my days all that he has to teach me.

8

School

When the paediatrician who diagnosed Simon told us that there was a long, hard road ahead of us, I was far too dazed fully to understand what he meant. Mercifully. A healthy mind, intent on survival, tries to deal with great shocks in such a way as to safeguard that survival. It refuses, initially, to accept all the implications of the disaster, only allowing their entry a few at a time, thereby giving itself a chance to adjust gradually. Months had changed into years before I had any real idea of the meaning of that phrase, spoken by someone who knew, from personal experience, every inch of the way.

The question of Simon's education had raised its head long before the diagnosis, before either of us had any clear idea that there was anything wrong with him. Convinced that my husband's private and public school education had been superior to my own grammar school one, we had decided to "go private", and put Simon's name down for one of the local private preparatory schools. This entailed visiting the school, and talking to the headmaster and his wife. Perhaps there was some premonition of the truth in my reactions: I found the whole experience very unreal. It seemed to have absolutely no relevance to the life of my quiet, apathetic little son who was then only two years old. I had not very much liked the school in question, but remained curiously and uncharacteristically disinclined to argue about it. Simon's name was duly placed at the bottom of the list.

Simon was rising four when the facts finally emerged, and, shocked and bewildered though we were, we nonetheless realized that we would have to act quickly if we were to find a suitable school for him. The trouble was that we had no idea what was and was not suitable for his particular presentation of the autistic handicap, nor what schools existed or where they were to be found. Feverishly, we wrote off to the two societies, the National Society for Mentally Handicapped Children, and the smaller, and more recently formed National Society for Autistic Children. The former sent us a long list of schools and units existing for the education of mentally handicapped children, out of which, trained in literary analysis though we both were, we could make little sense. There seemed to be no way of ascertaining which were able not just to contain autistic children, but actually to educate them. The reply from the NSAC was shorter, but far more revealing. There was, it seemed, only one school in the entire country which catered exclusively and positively for autistic children, and that was the Society School, as it was then called, at Florence Road, Ealing in London. It had been founded four years previously by a group of desperate and determined parents, who in fact became the National Society for Autistic Children. They had enlisted the services of Sybil Elgar, an infinitely experienced teacher with a genius for working with autistic children, and the success of her methods had already attracted the attention of psychiatrists, social workers, teachers and school inspectors from all over the country. Already the Society was planning to open another school at Gravesend, to be run on the same lines, but at the time of our need it was not yet open.

This was in 1966 – twenty-three years after Leo Kanner had first defined the syndrome he named "early infantile autism". There were, we understood from our reading, between four and five thousand school-age autistic children in Britain, yet nothing, it seemed, had been done by the State to provide for their education. To us it did not seem possible, or even believable, but such was the case. And the reason, we discovered, was that the Ministry of Education at the time refused to regard autism as a separate handicap, so that it did not qualify for special schools, as did the blind, the deaf or the spastic – and this despite the fact that there were roughly as many autistic children in the country as there were blind. Consequently, the educational policy was to fit autistic children into already existing structures, such as ESN schools, training centres, units for maladjusted children, or, if such establishments could not contain them, to relegate them to mental sub-normality hospitals.

Very few local education authorities knew anything whatsoever about autism, yet most were unwilling to admit their ignorance. An acquaintance of mine, a fellow member of the society, told me how her child had been interviewed for placement by the appropriate sub-committee, one of whose members had brought her dog along to the meeting. As the child, like Simon, had an obsessive terror of dogs, he became uncontrollable. The mother's request that the dog should be shut outside the room was regarded as evidence of her neurotic state, and the meeting was closed. If that mother had not been totally determined, and aware of her rights, the child would have spent the rest of his days in hospital, instead of improving visibly in the school place she eventually won for him with the help of more enlightened supporters.

Yet even in those early days it was known that autistic children, although they could not be cured, benefited from special education, sometimes to the point where they could be allowed to strike out independently into the world, to live and work amid the rest of us. All deteriorated once they were sent to mental sub-normality hospitals, where under-staffing precluded the individual attention they required in order to improve.

What the education authorities failed to understand then – as many still do today – was that the requirements of the autistic child are different from those of the mentally retarded, the mongoloid or the maladjusted. The type of teaching which achieves the best results, as has been demonstrated over the years by the success of the various Society schools, has to be geared to their special difficulties, with a programme structured and planned to take account of their specific handicaps. Fitting them into existing structures, which have not been designed with them in mind, is simply not facing up to the realities of the problem.

Today, in 1977, the general picture has improved a little, but the basic obstacle to real progress is still there: the Department of Education and Science does not, any more than its predecessor, recognize autism as a separate handicap. On the other hand, thanks largely to the steady and ever increasing work of the National Society for Autistic Children, many more local education authorities, and many more members of the general public are aware of the problem. Some 50–55 local education authority units for autistic children have been opened throughout the country, a few in cooperation with the NSAC, which itself is now responsible for the control of five independent schools, while local societies affiliated to the NSAC have opened another eight. In all, about a quarter of the estimated four to five thousand school-age autistic children are now receiving education geared to their needs. In case, however, these figures give rise to too much optimism, it is as well to note that out of ninety-four education authorities circularized by the NASC in 1975, no less than thirty-seven replied that they had neither any special provision for autistic children, nor any plans for provision in the future. The whole of Wales, for instance, sports only two schools.

This can hardly be called lightning progress, especially when the need is so crying, so proved by psychiatrists and teachers, and the distress so acute.

Even so, it is still better to be born autistic in 1977 than it was in 1966, the year that we first faced the prospect of finding a school for Simon.

Our first instinct was to turn to the Ealing school and apply for a place, even though we knew there would be at least forty applications for each one available – and there were only two or three, for the school was small. We were not successful that first time, but were heartened by being told by Mrs Elgar that our own county was one of the first to be opening a unit for autistic children in the near future, and that Simon would certainly be offered a place in it. So we went away disappointed, because it had been immediately obvious to us how much the school had to offer, but far from despairing.

Sure enough, shortly afterwards, Simon and I were summoned for interviews at the local Child Guidance Clinic. The educational psychologist gave him a variety of tests, though she did not reveal her conclusions, and we both had an interview with the psychiatrist. My main recollected impression of those meetings is of their impersonality. I put on a very passable performance as the mother who has fully accepted and is coping with her handicapped child, and Simon, whilst he did not show any urge to communicate, did his best to perform what was required of him. No one probed any deeper. I was told in terms of great optimism of the new experimental unit for autistic children. It was due to open the following Autumn, as soon as the purpose-built building was finished. It was, unfortunately, some distance from our home, but transport, I was assured, would be provided.

We returned home with my feelings in a curious state of confusion. On the one hand the immediate problem of schooling for Simon appeared to be miraculously solved, which was a great boost to the morale, but on the other there persisted this odd feeling that we had not been talked to as people, that no one had betrayed any real compassion, but that instead we were cases, a pair of walking problems. It was an unpleasant and hurtful feeling. None of my private anxieties had found the light of day, none of the questions I desperately wanted to ask about Simon and his future had forced its way past the barrier of impersonality. We had just been pushed into a little drawer, with a label marked "solved" round our necks.

As things turned out, we were very, very far from being that. I shall probably never really know just what went wrong behind the scenes at that unit. Suffice it to say that everything that could, did. The transport, the essential link between the inevitably far-flung homes of the four autistic children who were to be the first intake, had obviously received minimal attention from the official responsible, and it was left to the caretaker of the school to which the unit was attached to drive round the county collecting them in a battered old car which was a dubious candidate for an MOT test. This process swallowed up some three hours of the school day, and left the children in a poor physical state for the training to be imposed upon them. When, later, the unit acquired a minibus, it did not come to the children's homes, but picked them up from the training centre in the nearby large town, where they had been deposited by the training centre's own coach. We did not begin to get really angry until we discovered that, without our knowledge, the minibus had often failed to pick up Simon at all, and that he had spent the entire school day at the training centre.

This was far from being the only drawback as far as we were concerned. The four children in the unit were of widely varying degrees of handicap. One was extremely severely disturbed, and inevitably the constant attention of the teacher had to be given to him. Our quiet, docile Simon consequently received very little. It was hard to accept, one day when I was visiting the unit, seeing the badly disturbed child banging Simon's head against the wall, hard enough to daze him, before the teacher could reach him. I liked and respected that teacher, but I could see that she had an impossible task. She admitted as much herself, and became very depressed.

It was not many months before we realized that somehow we would have to extricate ourselves from the drawer, and tear off the label marked "solved". This is far harder than getting oneself into the drawer in the first place. Simon did his bit by being sick every time he rode in the minibus, which was hardly surprising in view of the length of the journey. At least the resultant pallor, poor appetite and weight loss enabled me to enlist the help of our ever-sympathetic family doctor, who in turn wrote to the County Officer for Health, no mean ally. The problem was that if Simon did not attend the unit, there was nowhere else that was entirely suitable for him to go.

Various suggestions were put to me. They included having a Home Tutor, which I turned down flat, knowing full well that Home Tutors are not experienced in the teaching of autistic children, and being convinced, in any case, that Simon needed the experience of school possibly more than any other child I knew. Another idea was that I should try the local independent schools, to see if they felt they could take on a child such as ours. I duly visited a couple, and came away laughing at the ignorance that had prompted such a suggestion. Neither of the respective heads knew a thing about autism, yet they were both willing to take the child. Neither asked me any relevant questions concerning his behaviour. In both cases, he would have been one of a class of twenty-five or so children, taught by only partly qualified teachers.

I did not really feel like laughing, nor did my husband.

We returned to the charge with the Education Authority, for whom we were by now something of a headache. We did not actually *say* the thoughts that were in our minds, or the threats – but no doubt these showed in our voices. Eventually our persistence was rewarded and, after a great deal of dithering (not on our side), Simon was given a place in a small unit for maladjusted children attached to an ESN school some six miles from our home. We had already been to visit it, and had realized that it was by far the best compromise that we could all come to.

True, the unit was not geared to the special needs of autistic children, but it held several distinct advantages over the experimental one where Simon had been so unhappy. Perhaps the chief of these was the personality of the headmaster of the main ESN school, a man respected throughout the county for his vigorous, outspoken championship of the children's rights. He had a way with petty officialdom which filled me with admiration. Needless to say, there was no nonsense with transport where *his* school was concerned – a coach came daily to our door to pick up Simon, who joined some thirty other children on it.

The maladjusted children were housed in a separate building close to one side of the main school, and linked to it by a covered way. There were two classes of ten children, one senior and one junior. The classrooms were bright, filled with paintings, models, nature specimens and other samples of the children's work. The atmosphere was busy and purposeful, the activities guided by an experienced and caring teacher. I always loved visiting Simon's classroom.

Despite their varied handicaps and problems, the children were expected to conform to the discipline of the school, and nearly all did respond to that expectation. From the day he first went there, Simon's social behaviour showed a gradual but marked improvement. He also began, to our delight, to talk more.

The school was situated on the edge of the tough end of the town. Consequently many deprived and distressed children, as well as the physically and mentally handicapped, found their way to its shelter. And it was a shelter. The children, I think, were aware of it. That big, burly headmaster with his deep voice and dictatorial manner was totally devoted to them, and both they and their teachers were caught up in this devotion, which created a very special atmosphere. Towards the outside world, the head turned an aggressive, sometimes belligerent front – I would not have found it easy to confront him as, say, a magistrate in court, or as an education committee member trying to persuade him to accept some restriction on his school – but towards his children the force of his personality was exerted only to encourage, to stimulate, and to protect. I have seen children, mute where everyone else was concerned, answer him. For me, it was a most moving experience to attend the school's Christmas party, for instance, and to see the most withdrawn, the most physically unattractive, the most disturbed children come out of their shells, and join in the games and the dancing. In no other school, private, public, State, junior or senior have I seen such beautiful Christmas decorations, arranged with such care and taste.

For parents, he was not an easy head to deal with. He had seen too many feckless, prejudiced, uncaring examples of parenthood in his long years of teaching – some of them were even ex-pupils of his own school – for him to entertain much beyond gloomy suspicion towards them. He knew what poverty was, for he had to teach its fruits. He knew what the loss of self-respect entailed, for he had to grapple with its results, and try to save them. And he stood firmly all the time on their side, the side of the poor and underprivileged. "Well, Mr and Mrs Lovell, and what do you think of *your* son coming to an ESN school?" was his unpromising greeting to us when we arrived in his office for the first time, with our cultured middle-class voices, and well-cut clothes. But I had already seen round his school, and felt the atmosphere, and was not going to be rebuffed. It represented as much a haven for Simon as it did for the most ill-clad child there. I knew, if no one else did, that Simon was poorer than the poorest the moment he stepped away from the protection of our home – and homes, like any other human institution, are subject to decay. And I was positive, from the moment I saw him smile at the headmaster, that he would be happy in that school.

He was. For the next three years or so, he went off daily in the school coach, which stopped at our door. He went off willingly and happily to join children whom he soon learned to call by their names, to the care of a teacher who began to figure largely in the phrases he was coming out with more and more often. I, too, grew to know the school, for it was near enough to visit without too much difficulty, and parents were regularly invited to attend its functions. Only a few ever came. Most were working. I liked going – it gave me the feeling that I still had a share in Simon's development, and meeting his schoolfellows and teachers helped when it came to trying to prompt him to converse with me when at home. As I had actually seen his work in class, it was easier to get him to try to tell me about it.

There were two main drawbacks to this happy experience. Both of them were significant.

The first was that the school being at a distance from our home, with its pupils living some distance apart, meant that Simon completely lost any day-to-day contact with others of his own age group who attended neighbourhood schools, and who had been around when he was a toddler. An ESN school was a totally unknown quantity to my friends and acquaintances. Most of them had never set eyes on one, if they knew what it was, or whom exactly it was for. As I grew to know other parents from the school they confided in me that their children actually suffered insult and worse at the hands of their "normal" neighbours: "they went to the school for loonies didn't they?" Something is very amiss in an education system which permits the existence of this kind of isolation and ignorance. It is a very far cry indeed from the ideal of comprehensive schooling.

The second drawback, which did not worry us at first, was to increase in size and importance as time went by. Simon was in a class of ten children, in the charge of one teacher. Although, in comparison with classes in normal schools, this is a high teacher-pupil ratio, it is still not high enough for an autistic child. None of the other children was autistic, though all were disturbed to various degrees and for various reasons in their behaviour. The teacher was dedicated and experienced, and armed with the requisite diploma for teaching handicapped children – but she was not a specialist on the subject of autism. Simon's behaviour and difficulties puzzled her, and she was candid enough to say so. He was reading fairly fluently when he went to the school, for instance, and he was still reading fairly fluently when he left it three years later, but with no significant increase in comprehension. Writing and number work defeated both him and the teacher almost completely. His creative work, on the other hand, did improve. He seemed to enjoy it greatly – producing strange pictures which gave me some of my first insights into the manner of his vision of the world. I do not know any other child, for instance, who draws a horse *from above*, i.e. from the rider's eye level.

Simon did. He always tried to draw exactly what he saw, however unusual the angle.

In the end his teachers could no longer overlook these difficulties. I had my head firmly buried in the sand, and so was taken unawares when the headmaster sent for me and told me, very gently, that he did not think that his school would be suitable for Simon at secondary level. He suggested that we begin to look around for somewhere else. By this time I knew the facts – we had not been members of the National Society for six years for nothing – and the facts were that with one exception there *was* no suitable alternative. I told him so. The tightness of my voice spoke more eloquently than my words. I can still remember his silence and the compassion in his eyes. Interviews such as these must have been one of the hardest parts of his job. Diffidently, he suggested the Steiner schools. I did not leap at the idea, chiefly because of the distance of the schools from our home, and also partly because I was convinced that autistic children develop their potential better when they are not mixed with other forms of handicap. The success of the Society school was sufficient proof to me.

The world seemed to be crumbling again. I had felt very secure while Simon was going daily to the local school, as I am sure he felt so himself. It seemed hard to uproot him. He was able to play a part in family life as his routine was similar to that of the other children, and this in turn helped the practical side of running the family. A small comfort was that if we really found ourselves in despair, unable to find any other suitable school, the headmaster would not have actually turned Simon out – he was not that kind of man – but it would have been unfair to him, as well as to Simon, if we did not do our best to find an alternative.

It was difficult to know where to start – the more so as by this time I had three other children to look after. I made some enquiries about the CARE (Cottage and Rural Enterprises) villages for the mentally handicapped, and went to talk to Peter Forbes, who organizes them. Simon, of course, was too young for this type of community life as yet, but it was beginning to dawn on me that we needed to look further ahead than we had done hitherto. School-leaving age, although it was still six years or so off, had begun to assume an ominous significance. It may seem neurotic to worry about events so far in the future, but I knew that I had to. From my reading, I knew that autistic children do not stop developing at sixteen, they continue far longer than normal children. To give them special education for so many years only to discontinue it at an arbitrary date which has no relevance whatsoever to their needs seemed to me all but criminal. It would have been kinder to do nothing from the start.

Then, as if instinctively turning to the oasis in the desert, though with no real hope of ever reaching it, we sent in our second application to the Society School at Ealing – applications can be made afresh each time a vacancy occurs, since success depends not on any sort of merit, but on the current balance of severely and less severely handicapped children in the school. Once again, we took Simon along for interview, and I tried not to want too hard that he should obtain a place. Ever since our first visit, six years previously, I had longed for him to be taught by Mrs Elgar. I knew that if anyone could teach him, she could: that through long experience, sensitive observation, and natural gift, there was little she did not know about the idiosyncrasies of this strange handicap, and absolutely nothing about its victims that repelled her. It was obvious that she loved the children, and that her unique combination of love, skill and experience could elicit responses where others failed. The interview was a tense experience.

Providence, once again, took a hand. Two weeks later a letter arrived to say that this time Simon had been given a place. I could not believe it. I cried and cried – but out of relief and joy. Life in general was not very easy just then, and here, at least, was one miraculously bright spot. Simon was safe, in the safest place he could possibly be, with the best teacher I knew. He was to start at the school as a day boy the following term. Our education authority agreed to pay the fees – as one of the more compassionate authorities in the country they agree that if they themselves cannot provide the facilities for their handicapped children, they can at least ensure that the children can benefit from these facilities when they exist elsewhere. Not all have such an attitude, and we were and still are grateful. Fortunately, another child in the county, living within five miles from us, attended the same school, so that Simon's transport involved no extra cost.

All the same, as the time for the change drew near, I began

to grow apprehensive. Simon was older now, and more aware of the pattern of his life. It is a big upheaval for a normal child to change school, a child who is articulate, and who can understand the reasons for the change. I could not help being sad at having to impose this incomprehensible burden on Simon, at wrenching him away from the safety of familiar faces and routines, to drop him into a completely new world. His utter defencelessness struck me more than ever.

Everyone, however, was agreed, from his headmaster and the education authority, to ourselves, that the change was definitely for his good. It had to be done.

I tried to prepare him, but as it was very difficult to gauge how much he understood of anything so abstract as the future, I could not be sure that I succeeded at all. "Simon go to new school next term," he would repeat placidly after me, without the slightest trace of alarm.

When the day came, he went off peaceably in the taxi he was to share with the other child, leaving me to wander round the house, unable to settle to anything, or think of anyone but him. He returned home looking as if nothing untoward had happened, and, with a sigh of relief, I relaxed a little.

Not, however, for long. The changes which took place in him during that new term were visible. The first was a new and plainly marked reluctance to go to school. He could not tell me about it, but he demonstrated it very efficiently by staging a go-slow at breakfast time. Until then, I had never experienced the slightest difficulty with him over meals – he seemed to like all foods indiscriminately, and was always hungry. If anything, he has proved the easiest of my four children to feed – by no means the case with many autistic children. Now, breakfast began to assume a distinctly nightmarish quality. He would not eat, except at a pace a snail would have found slow, he would not look at us, and he often cried silently. In the end, thoroughly worried, I phoned Mrs Elgar about it. I remember hearing the smile in her voice. "He's having to work for the first time in his life," she told me, "and he's none too enthralled about it. Give him time, and don't worry." Somewhat reassured, I decided to take no notice of this breakfast performance. If he did not finish in time to go out to meet the car, I ruthlessly sent him off regardless. He was a big boy for his age, and growing fast. The resultant hunger put the message across far more forcefully than any words. By the end of his first term, breakfast had returned to normal.

The second change, much more important, was a distinct maturing of personality. He seemed to be growing far more aware of himself. He even – and this was a totally new development – began occasionally to take a stand against authority. Helping me in the house at that time was Marianne, the last of a long line of *au pair* girls. She was Swiss, and, like all the Swiss girls who ever came to us, an excellent help, with a very sweet, gentle and shy personality. Unfortunately, she was not endowed with any natural authority, and suddenly, of all the unexpected crises, our quiet, docile Simon began to defy and flout her exactly as any normal eleven year old boy would undoubtedly have done. Time after time I would return from shopping or from a school run to find Marianne in tears, and Simon flatly refusing to come in out of the rain, or to go to bed, or to stay near her when on the Common, riding his bike. I was secretly delighted, though I could hardly show this in front of Marianne. His constant docility had always worried me – it was as if he were absolutely unable to move without the assent of another person. Now here he was at last sticking up for himself. He did not show signs of rebellion against me. Perhaps it would have been better if he had, but on the other hand I am not sure that I could have coped with them very adequately, particularly at that time. My husband was very seldom at home just then, and we were both under great strain.

Gradually I saw Simon adjusting to the new efforts required of him. He began to settle down, and to make unmistakable progress. By the end of his second term, Mrs Elgar was very pleased with him. I was amazed at the improvement in his writing and his number work – the two subjects the teachers had despaired of at the ESN school. The only drawback, as far as I was concerned, was the difficulty I found in visiting the school. Ealing is nearly thirty miles from our home, separated from us by heavily congested roads. With the three younger children to care for, and a large amount of ferrying to and fro to be done, the journey could only be fitted into daily routine with great effort. I never attended any school function, and regretted and missed this greatly. It meant that I no longer felt involved in Simon's life to the same extent, and this was hard. This however was my personal problem rather than Simon's, or so it seemed. We had been miraculously lucky, and it would have been ingratitude to quibble.

For, hopeless as the general picture had seemed when we first learned of the diagnosis, we ourselves had always found hope. When we had been forced, as most are, to squeeze Simon into existing structures, he had at least profited from them, if only for a time. And, before it was too late, he was receiving the specialized teaching he needed. Simon is one of the happy few. It is a fact never to be forgotten.

If it is true, as I think it is, that there is a pattern to our lives, then the increase of happiness and stability that came to me through Simon's attendance at the Society school was no coincidence. I needed it absolutely, for other problems, still more pressing, even more momentous, claimed my whole attention. The fact that Simon was settled and happy, receiving the best possible teaching, developing all his potential under expert guidance, gave me a breathing space, the chance I needed to think my way with less hysteria through the shaking structure of the rest of my world.

9

Desert Places

Any reader of average perspicacity will have noticed that in this account so far I have tended to use the first person singular far more than the first person plural when referring to the parental role. This is not wholely egocentricity. There is another reason.

Although the incidents recounted in the previous chapters occurred while there were still two of us, for the last four years I have been in the position of having to carry the responsibilities of this role alone. Recovery from the shattering blow of the breakdown of our marriage is, I know now, real, but it is still comparatively recent. Scars remain, and are still tender. Perhaps they are there for good, and will always be so. It is no simple thing to survive rejection. Most of the bitterness and anger is, however, spent. What remains is, I know, centred around the figure of Simon.

This is what has made it very difficult to use the pronoun "we" when writing this book. Everything which in the past I had thought we experienced as a united couple, especially before and after the diagnosis of Simon, was falsified by the newly discovered fact that all along we had not been united at all. The unity had only existed in my own eyes and mind. So that when I try to describe what happened I find I can only do so honestly when I write of my own thoughts and feelings, for, in the light of subsequent events, they could not have been those of my ex-husband.

Our marriage did not die suddenly. The agony was prolonged over a period of four years. Someone, a film director, I think, once wrote that his idea of hell was of being shut up for perpetuity with someone you love who has ceased to love you. I would add as a rider that the torment can be greatly increased if you have shared very profound experiences and responsibilities, such as childbirth, or the care of a handicapped child, so that the happiness and wellbeing of others depends on the resuscitation of that dead emotion.

Basically, I am, always have been, and probably now always will be an optimist. When I realized, soon after the court hearing that made David's advent to the family permanent, that the relationship between Paul and myself was suddenly deteriorating to the point where any real communication between us was already all but impossible, I jumped for safety to the conclusion that we had fallen into the oft-discussed "middle life crisis", when the partners in most marriages find that they have to readjust to the reality of the drudgery, routine and emotional wear and tear that is unavoidable in bringing up a family. Even holding tight to this, however, I was frightened enough to think that we needed help – but once again, I had no idea where to go for it. I could not visualize my extremely intellectual husband agreeing to visit a marriage guidance counsellor. Instinctively, I turned to my doctor, who had already helped me through so much, and poured out my worries through yet another unfair share of his surgery time. He prescribed a policy of tranquillizers and patience. He was undoubtedly right in the first, since I had to care for four children, but I have at times questioned his wisdom in the second. Waiting and hoping could not help us: the problem was too deep and too complicated for that. If the crash was to be averted at all, we needed expert help then and there, such as I only found later – but even that might not have served, since not all such problems are soluble. If that *were* so, and I suspect that such was our case, the patience was no bad thing for it permitted the marriage to endure until the children were old enough to make caring for them less physically demanding.

For three and a half years I shut my eyes to all evidence to the contrary, and pinned my hopes entirely on the belief that this increasingly painful situation was one that could be healed by time. I was, had I but realized it, putting on a repeat performance of my behaviour when I knew that there was something crucially wrong with Simon, but had denied the knowledge both to my conscious self and to the world at large.

And the effect of this two-level emotional life was almost identical: increased nerviness and irritability, indigestion, sleeplessness – all of which did absolutely nothing to improve the situation. I loved Paul deeply, and I clung to that love and to my belief in its eventual victory, as a swimmer in choppy waters clings to a broken spar: I was afraid I would drown without it.

Once, in the days before Simon, I had believed ardently in the supremacy of the human mind. That belief had disintegrated. But I still had another: I firmly believed, romantic that I was, in the power and endurance of human love. Brought up for years in the "Let me not to the marriage of true minds" school, I had staked, as I thought, my whole life on that ideal. I could not, I was sure I could not, afford to lose it. There had to be some brightness to live for.

So I stuck my head in the sand with all the force I had. The sand, however, was a poor protection against the chilly courtesy that had taken the place of tenderness, though at least it had the advantage of effectively preventing clear-sightedness. Like the medically prescribed patience, in the long run this was probably a help.

Instinctively, as much for our own pride's sake as for the children's, we made great efforts to preserve our public image of being a harmonious, well-integrated family – though, at least in my case, not without much pain. The truth was so very far from the appearances. All but our very closest family were taken in. I often wonder how much the children sensed of their parents' hypocrisy. Probably most of it. They showed signs of strain. Joanna was quiet and repressed, Tom was developing a stammer, David was perpetually over-excited – but Simon just smiled on us all. The nuances of emotion were not for him.

In the last year, pretence became all but impossible. The courtesy suddenly became ice. There is a short poem by Robert Frost which beautifully describes his reaction to ice:

> Some say the world will end in fire,
> Some say in ice.
> From what I've tasted of desire
> I hold with those who favour fire.
> But if it had to perish twice,
> I think I know enough of hate

To say that for destruction ice
Is also great
And would suffice

It was destroying me, and I knew it. It was also threatening
the children through me. I became hysterical. I felt that I was
in a trap and I could see no way out. Either I tried to carry
on in this state of daily pain, holding the marriage together
with my own skin, until I broke down mentally (and I felt I
was near to that) in the which case they would be left without
a mother, or I deliberately broke the marriage up by asking
my husband to go, which would not only make them fatherless,
but would leave us exposed and vulnerable on every side –
financially, emotionally, even physically. For me it would
mean looking after the household and children entirely on my
own, as there was no family to help, and Marianne had completed her year with us and returned home.

I felt that I had built the trap myself through the flaws in
my own personality. I had done everything wrong, nothing
right. Inevitably the image of Simon loomed in my mind, for
the first time as an image of failure, to be succeeded by that of
little David, whom I had so blindly, so stupidly dragged into all
this unhappiness, taking from him his last chance of security
and stability. Wildly, my mind ran round and round this trap,
round and then round again. There had to be another way out,
but I could not find it.

I was more frightened than I had ever been in my life. At
last there was no more place for pride. I was beaten and on
my knees. All I wanted was to rest, to get out, away, anywhere,
anyhow. Every ideal I had ever had was now gone. Human
love was as fallible as the human brain. There was nothing left
to live for – except the victims of my folly: the children. The
thought of them made me pause. I could not just leave them
to rot because I myself had failed. What would become of
them, and especially of Simon? I could not let him down, betray
his trust. However much I had failed them and him in the past
by not living up to their father's needs, at least now there was
one clear course of action I could and must take: I must work
to mitigate the effects of that failure. Which left me no option.
In order to work, I had first to survive. Appeals to Paul had
proved useless, for no link was left to carry the urgency of the

message. Despair was unseen. It was up to me. I went to see a solicitor.

Some weeks later, every nerve strung tight, I asked Paul to go. I told him I could not live with him any longer – on his terms. I shall never forget his look of surprise. Deep inside me, I still did not believe that he would choose to end it all, that he would actually pack, walk out of the house, and leave the five of us to fend for ourselves. I could not accept reality.

We were due to attend a big school Guy Fawke's night party with the children two days later, and we agreed that he would leave the day after that, that we would do this one thing together for the last time as a family. As I watched the flames leaping up from that bonfire, I felt they were symbolic. Our strained, miserable faces glowed in the light, while the children shouted with excitement. It was a holocaust, reducing all but a thread of my life to ashes.

Next day, he moved out. I spent the afternoon at a friend's house so that I should not be there when he took his things. I did not care what he took. He had already destroyed everything I had that I prized. But – not quite everything. I returned to find empty spaces on the walls and bookshelves, an empty bed, and an empty place at the table. I had half an hour before the children came home from school. Feverishly, I ran round moving books and pictures, filling up the gaps, setting the tea things on the smaller table in the kitchen, removing the extra chairs. The material structure that made up the safe boundaries of their world had to stay the same. I must not give way. I had to keep things ticking over. Tears must wait, or so I thought. It was not until some time later that I found how much comfort we could find in sharing our grief, in showing our real feelings to each other.

The children had all been told, as simply as possible, what had happened. I had not been able to face telling Simon without some support and advice as to how to go about it, and had been to ask for help from the psychiatrist specializing in autistic children whom I had met through the National Society for Autistic Children, whose sane, practical yet compassionate approach I knew I could trust. He recommended that I should stick to concrete facts, for they were all that Simon could cope with.

Telling Simon those concrete facts was one of the most

agonizing tasks I have ever yet been given. So much misery boiled down to so few words: "Daddy's gone away, Simon. He doesn't live here any more. He lives in London now with another lady. He'll come to see you at the weekend."

"Daddy's gone away," he repeated, in a puzzled voice, "Daddy doesn't live here any more. Daddy lives in London with another lady. Come at the weekend." Then he said it again, as if to make sure he had got it right. I had not bargained for autistic obsessiveness. He continued to repeat it for the rest of the day, and the next, and the next, and for weeks to come. Each repetition twisted the knife further. For the rest of us there was no chance of forgetting, none of escape. We just had to listen.

Divorce, if the breaking of the relationship is one-sided, as it was in our case, is for the deserted half of the couple very akin to bereavement. The process of mourning, which is essential to recovery, has to pass through several stages. It is more complicated, however, than bereavement in that the succession of these stages is constantly being interrupted by the reappearance of the lost partner, alive, well, and possibly rejoicing in his or her freedom. These interruptions make recovery slower, and, I think, far more difficult.

In our case, for the children's feelings seemed to follow the same pattern as my own, the first days of shock, numbness and bursts of feverish activity were followed by unrestrainable grief and severe depression. I became very frightened by the violence of my feelings – I was afraid of going mad, or, worse still, of hurting the children. This time I was determined to find professional help; I knew now that I could not get through this alone. Medical channels turned out to be blind alleys. The help I needed came indirectly, through a friend of a friend who had passed through the same straits and survived, thanks to an NSPCC social worker who had helped her.

Few know – I certainly did not – that the National Society for the Prevention of Cruelty to Children run a service of counselling in cases of "marital disharmony", rightly believing that if you help the parents, you help the children. I baulked at first at the idea of approaching them: the name for me held associations of battered babies and general violence to children, but my need was too great for such inhibitions to stand for long, and soon after I phoned up the area office. That was how I came to find the first real support I had known in years, for the social worker I spoke to, and who came to see me, is probably one of the most experienced, the most skilled, and the most shrewd in the whole country, as well as being the least afraid of human emotion. There are very few people who can teach you with sympathy, accuracy *and humour* to recognize your feelings for what they are, so as to enable you to re-channel anger out of its destructive course inwards, against the self where it can do nothing but harm, and to turn it outwards, against less vulnerable objects, so that it strengthened instead of diminishing that bruised and bleeding patient, the ego. He was never impatient with me when I phoned him, however busy he might have been with other work, and however hysterically I began the phone call, I always ended it laughing. He says now that I would have come through the experience without his help, though it would have taken longer. I am sure that I could not have done so, and for this once I stick to my own judgment.

That help I regard as fundamental to recovery, but by itself it could not have led me to the other kind of life I now lead. It simply opened my eyes. Other help, such as I had never known before, came from all quarters, from the most unexpected sources. People who had hitherto been mere acquaintances became caring friends, caring enough to ring up every day to give me a chance to talk, to show that they wanted to help. Not all the approaches were tactful, and I was as sensitive as if I had been flayed, but the important thing was that they were made. It was not easy to learn to live as a single woman again, after fourteen years of marriage. Perhaps it was the other single women, those who had never married, who helped me most here, for they took quite for granted difficulties which I tended to get out of perspective. But all the help is symbolized for me by the cherished memory I have of returning from a walk with the children one Sunday afternoon to find a home-baked blackcurrant pie in a bag hanging from the handle of my front door. There was no message with it, and it was some days before I discovered the donor, who had walked several miles to leave it: it was my doctor's receptionist. If I cried then, it was not from misery, or self-pity, but from the birth of a new kind of warmth inside me. I had discovered the existence of a different sort of love from the one I had believed in until then, less dramatic, less turbulent than the love between man and woman, but with a power of its own which I was now experiencing for the first time.

If I have described the beginnings of my own recovery first, it is because that of the children depended upon it to a very large extent. It was only when I learned not to be ashamed of my anger, but to acknowledge it, that they could come to terms with theirs. I encouraged them to talk about their feelings, and above all I reassured them again and again that it was through no fault of theirs that Daddy had gone. Even so, they were showing sufficient signs of disturbance and depression for me to decide that they, too, needed more expert help than I could give them. I am not obsessive about psychiatrists – it must be realized that I had absolutely no family to advise me, and, certainly at first, the weight of the responsibility I had been left with was too much to carry alone. I was all too aware of the dangers that beset children of broken families. I wanted mine to receive all possible support. Through my doctor, I obtained an appointment at a big London children's hospital, where, together with the children, I saw a team of psychiatrist and social worker. In the event, we did not need to go very frequently, though we do still go from time to time. I am certain the visits helped the children, just as they helped me in my approach to them. They, just as much as I, experienced this tremendous need to talk, and to go on talking about their feelings, without fear of shocking or overburdening, to a disinterested third party. We could not have borne it all alone. We could not always burden friends with this mess of emotion. We had to have somewhere to turn.

There was, in fact, somewhere else, but at that stage we still had not found it. Perhaps we weren't quite ready for it. But we began to be active again. The work of re-adjustment had begun.

The three younger children had all had to change schools. They found themselves suddenly dropped into the State system, which turned out to be the best thing that could have happened to them. The change from their previous environment helped to lift depression, whilst the freer atmosphere helped them to relax. They began, as it were, to swim. A constant stream of creative work came home, to delight us all. They could not have had more caring teachers.

We joined a judo club. I had thought somewhat vaguely that this was a good, healthy and cheap masculine-type activity which might stimulate the boys, as well as being of some practical value in this world of violent playgrounds. I was somewhat surprised by Joanna's keenness to join as well, but absolutely staggered by the way all three took to it in a matter of weeks. Now, three years, one club trophy, three green belts, many contests and sundry medals later, I look back on that initial vagueness with considerable amusement: I could not possibly have foreseen how much benefit the sport, about which I had known absolutely nothing, was to bring us. It definitely helped the boys achieve a measure of self-confidence which they might otherwise never have gained. The first couple of weeks they cried at the least knock. Nowadays tears are reserved for suitable occasions, such as being winded by a throw from the club ace. Joanna is renowned for the strength of her hold-downs – the muscles she has developed playing the 'cello stand her in good stead. And I vastly enjoy club nights as the occasion for a good laugh and chat with other parents, besides the pleasure of being a one-woman fan club.

Music, from being Simon's special therapy, became everyone's. Sufficient money was coming in to continue all the lessons – just. Everyone took pleasure in working, and pride in progressing. It provided not only an outlet for feelings, but also a purpose and a discipline, and a chance to achieve. I hoped that such a structure of work and play would arm them for the future, especially against the onset of teenage feelings of inadequacy and failure. Certainly it has helped up to the present stage.

But what of Simon in all this? How does he fit into this pattern of purposeful activity? The answer, if I am honest, is that he didn't. He couldn't. He was shut in with his confused feelings by the barriers of autism. There could be little expressing of feelings for him, for although he had them – I have seen him weeping silently – I do not know if he knew what those feelings were. I could not help him because to do so we needed the common language which we did not have. I grieved for him, and, perhaps for the first time in my relationship with him since his diagnosis, I felt bitter, bitter at being so powerless to help, and bitter at being placed in this agonizing position with him. It was through Simon that the full force of betrayal hit me. To me, Simon was a sacred trust.

Try as I might, I could not help him. The demands of the other children left me with little to spare. He could not join in the judo; he could only join in very little of the music. For the first time, I had to rely entirely on his school to give him what I no longer could. My role shrank into being merely a source of physical comfort. It did not seem much.

Naturally I had explained to Mrs Elgar all that had happened. She had been entirely kind, and sympathetic, and I knew I could trust her to take care of all that happened at the school end. Her firmness, skill and love would give him a continuity there which would help him more than my initial tears and panics at home, tears which he could not understand, much less comfort.

Throughout most of that first year of being a one-parent family, Simon merely co-existed with us, excluded from our innermost circle by the very intensity of our grief. The only perceptible change in him was that he tended to hang around me more, to touch me, or stroke my hair, as if to reassure himself that I was still there. In some ways his peaceableness, once the "Daddy's gone away"refrain died out, was a curious comfort to us. He was growing fast, and was already turning into a more solid figure in his place at table.

Every week or fortnight, my ex-husband came to take the children out for the day. They were glad to see him, and needed to do so, to be reassured that they still had a father who cared about them. But for me, these visits were a refined kind of torture. I was by no means cured of my love for him, and I felt that I never could be cured while I continued to see him. Each sight of him brought on a new, violent fit of depression. It was my solicitor who counselled me to find some neutral ground where I could leave the children in good hands and return to fetch them later, thus avoiding the now dreaded encounter.

It was clearly good advice, but where on earth was I to find such ideal "neutral ground", near enough to be within walking distance of home, trains etc.? And whoever would be willing to welcome four over-excited children into their homes twice every Sunday throughout the year? I racked my brains. Eventually it occurred to me that if anyone was likely to know of such a haven, it was the vicar of our local church, who would doubtless be in touch with many of the elderly people who lived around, and who might be prepared to help out when they learned the circumstances. I rang him up and, hesitantly, asked his help.

It was then that I met the act of kindness which was for me like the fitting of the final piece into a jig-saw puzzle. The vicar and his wife, although I had never so much as set foot in their church, offered to take the children for me themselves. When I protested, they merely said that Sunday was, in any case, the day when they were most tied to their home, and, as they already had four children of their own, four more would not make that much difference – the understatement of the year! My protests were easily overcome. The vicarage was ideally situated from the practical point of view – close to our home, and within walking distance of the station. I could hardly leave the children in safer hands.

I was extremely moved by the sheer simplicity with which that very considerable help was offered, as though it was the most natural thing in the world that it should be. Nobody uttered any sermons in my presence, but I witnessed help going out to others in all directions, in just the same way. The house was, of course, next door to the church – only a few steps away. It was not long before, self-consciously, embarrassed by my own easy tears, I made those steps, with the children behind me. We were made welcome. And we discovered – not just me, but each one of us – a whole new source of warmth and strength.

In my teens I had sneered at my mother, who, after years of conveniently neglecting the church, returned to it fervently during the long years of my father's fatal illness. It had all seemed to me too easy. I had called it clutching at straws. At university I had learned to call religion the opiate of the masses, the drug that dulled the reality of human existence. I had read Voltaire, Sartre, and disturbing, intoxicating renegades such as André Gide. I had regarded Christians as a humourless race, particularly those Protestants I had met in France and Switzerland – without knowing much of their history. In those days I was young, my pride was still undamaged, and I followed enthusiastically where the twentieth-century thinkers led, ecstatic in my idealization of humanity.

Now I was no longer young, and the paths I had followed had led me into a waste land. Nothing could possibly dull the reality of the experiences I had come through; I had lived every moment of it to the full. Once again, when I found that I could not bear it any more, I was left confronted by two options: one was to give up, and choose death, which was also the final failing of the children, and the other was to look, as it were, past the pain, and to turn it somehow, to some positive account – only this could not be done alone and unaided. Once I had made the steps which were the final renunciation of pride, I was ready to begin to look at the second option, to try to look at what had happened to us as a bridge towards other people, rather than as a fortress which shut us away from them. And in trying to do this, we found new strength, and much comfort.

The cynics will surely smile. It is all so obvious. We were under immense pressure. Like my mother, I was clutching at straws. Every church is full of silly women, holding on to empty lives. Yet in times of crisis, we usually stop laughing at them, for their strength is astonishing. And in my case, the straw proved to have the strength of a life-line. For the fact remains that we have discovered how to be happy again.

Contrary to the general pattern, the church in our area is not only alive, but flourishing – to the point where closed-circuit television has been installed, and there is talk of building extensions. As newcomers, we never were given the feeling that we were being done good unto. The community quietly and simply opened up and took us in. The long isolation was gone. People asked me how best they could help Simon. Seeing more of him, they began to lose some of their fear of him. I tried to explain to them how he could never understand metaphysics, for they are abstract, but that he could and did respond to love, which is their human interpretation. Substitute fathers appeared from all sides to give the children the horseplay and deep bass jokes they so sorely missed.

I am not trying to suggest that we underwent a sudden, mighty, road-to-Damascus conversion. We have not rushed to extremes, and become fanatics or militants, which would only have proved our continuing instability. What has happened has been a quiet, but growing thing, an ever-increasing sense of peace.

One of my chief fears, for instance, since becoming a lone parent, has been of dying suddenly. The fear is not of death in and for itself, though I am terrified of extreme physical pain, but of leaving the children overwhelmed by a second stupefying loss. There was no one ready or willing to step into my shoes, no one prepared to reassure me that they would consider doing so. The children had increased this fear by speaking of it, and by showing their anxiety if ever I chanced to be late home, or out driving in difficult conditions. Nowadays it is easier. It has not vanished, and I drive extremely defensively, but just as I have learned that there is a way of living through catastrophes, so I have learned to *trust* that a way would be found for them too, that they would not be destroyed. It is a matter of feeling that the burden is somehow shared.

This sense of peace, of new found warmth, has affected my relationship with my ex-husband. After the divorce was made absolute, he re-married and went to live abroad. No doubt the physical distance between us has helped, but much of the anger and bitterness towards him I find has now faded. Except in one respect. I do not think I can find it in my heart to forgive him for leaving Simon, nor do I think I ever shall. It would need a saint to forgive a hurt done to such as Simon, and I am no saint. It is possible to pardon a hurt done to oneself, but how can one pardon a hurt done to someone who is helpless?

I can, at least, try to understand. Statistics tell us that one in every four marriages ends in divorce. At the time of Simon's diagnosis, I would have said that it was impossible for ours to end that way, for we had exceptional bonds uniting us, and more tastes in common than the vast majority of couples. I was, as I have said, very naïve. Although I had picked up a good deal of second-hand psychology at university, I knew absolutely nothing about stress. It had never occurred to me that each individual reacts to it differently according to his or her personality, and that each has therefore a different breaking point, largely established by early experiences.

Because I myself had been able to tolerate the stresses of rearing a mentally handicapped child, in addition to the other stresses of married life – financial, physical and emotional, I assumed that my husband had also. In fact he had not, and what was worse, he felt unable to tell me so. Intent on nest-building, I flew to and fro without noticing the barrier that was growing between us. In the end, as the pressures on him increased, he found his options had decreased to either breaking or escaping. Other options, less drastic in their effect on the family, might perhaps have availed him, if only someone had helped him to find them. But the help he needed was never there, and he could not ask for it.

The birth of a mentally handicapped child into a family does not inevitably lead to the breakdown of the marriage. But it definitely imposes a terrific extra strain on it. I am certain that the stress could be lessened by perceptive, and, above all, continuous support. The couple can be helped to gauge the pressures on them, so that they can avoid incurring unnecessary ones which others, in more advantageous circumstances, can tolerate. Given such support, the marriage which carries a handicapped child could in some ways be said to be less at risk, for the parents learn to see themselves and their role as parents more clearly. And if they receive the extra help, the help that I have only found so recently, there is a chance that everything may fall into a different, less frightening, perspective.

We ourselves are now, irretrievably, a broken family. Yet, incredibly enough, we can still truthfully call ourselves a happy family. There are still days of aching recollection, days of apathy and isolation, days of misery, but they are widely spaced now, and when they do come I do not feel that the pit is bottomless, as I once did. For the most part, our house is full of music, and terrible school jokes, while every meal starts with the judo command "Hajime", meaning "Begin". It is not a closed-up house.

Had it not been for Simon, I am not sure that I would have had the will to survive. Simon has opened for me a succession of doors, doors which lead out of the prison of the self. When he first took me out into the world of the sick and the handicapped, I did not know it, but he was giving me the strength to make the next escape, which was harder since it had to be done alone, and self-pity and guilt are vigilant guards. And thanks to Simon, I found that the desert was not a desert at all, but simply a new world.

10

"As we grow older the world becomes stranger"

It was while Simon was settling in at the Society school at Ealing, before the storm described in the previous chapter finally broke, that I first heard of the Somerset Court project.

The same group of parents whose frustration, anger and determination had driven them to organize by themselves the education for their children which the State declined to provide, by setting up the Society school, today known as the Sybil Elgar School, were now finding, as their children grew older, that their problem had in fact been two-fold, and that they had only solved the first part of it – perhaps the easier part. The second now loomed large in front of them. Although the undoubted success of the Ealing school had led to the formation of many other similar schools and units throughout the country, no one had as yet taken on the problem of the children's future once they had passed school-leaving age. Although some of the original pupils had progressed to the point of being able to leave the Ealing school for normal schools, most had not, and, barring a miraculous remission of their disabilities, or the discovery of the cause and cure of the handicap of autism, were going to need some degree of shelter, if not total shelter, for the rest of their days. This, however, did not mean that they could not function as human beings – far from it. Provided that the special tuition and highly structured régime that had brought about their various degrees of improvement were continued, many could continue to improve and mature for many years, long after most normal children are considered to have stopped developing.

These were the facts, supported by research. The State, however, once more declined to face them. Existing structures were still deemed sufficient. By the time the children reached sixteen years of age, however, these had dwindled to two options: the senior workshops at the local Training Centres, if the children were sufficiently well adjusted socially, or, if they were not, the long-stay wards of the mental sub-normality hospitals. These, it has by now been sufficiently demonstrated, are not suitable environments for the autistic, and once forced into them, they swiftly deteriorate, even if they had previously benefited from years of special schooling. Such wastage of skill, effort, money, time and emotion hardly needs emphasizing. Independent organizations such as the Rudolph Steiner, or CARE communities offer a different form of solution, but both suffer from the drawback that they are not designed with the special problems of the autistic in view.

Thus the parents of the first children to have been educated at the Society school faced a blank as great, if not greater, than they had originally faced in 1962. But the progress their children had made under Mrs Elgar's teaching inspired them, and they were now in the way of being veteran campaigners. They set about organizing themselves with considerable efficiency. They formed a new charity, the Ealing Autistic Trust, which, though affiliated to the National Society for Autistic Children, had as its sole aim the foundation of a residential adolescent, and, eventually, adult community for autistic people. The foundation would start as a boarding school, with four school terms, holidays and long weekends at home, but would eventually, it was hoped, become fully residential for fifty-two weeks of the year.

In 1973, when I was almost totally preoccupied by my own miseries, the Trust was busy hunting for a suitable property, and for an equally suitable amount of financial support. Eventually, they found what they wanted: a fine large house set in twenty acres of grounds, in Somerset, only a couple of miles from the sea. Negotiations for purchase proved long and complicated, whilst the financial manoeuvres were – sophisticated. The members of the Trust, however, were no timid newcomers to the field of money-raising. By the Spring of 1974, the project had become reality. That August, Somerset Court opened to become the first community of its kind in the country. Mrs

Elgar had left the Society school to take on the herculean task of making the dream a viable, financially self-supporting concern. She was not above scrubbing the floors herself in those first, shoestring days. Her first group of pupils consisted mainly of old hands from the Society school, now the founder members of the new school.

There was everything to be done: grounds to be turned into profit-making market gardens, workshops to be set up so that soft toys, wickerwork, weaving, etc., could be made and sold, every possible money-making function to dream up and organize, as well as – vital, this, in the long term – ways of integrating the school into the local community. Only those who know Sybil Elgar (who was awarded the MBE in 1975, for her services to autistic children) can possibly appreciate how it is possible for so much to have been achieved in so short a time. For now, already, in 1977, Somerset Court is part of the Mendip scene, adopted by local charities, aided by voluntary work from villagers, and known, thanks to Sybil's tireless speech-making and presence at public functions, in towns and villages throughout the South West. So far it has survived escalating costs (1973, it may be remembered, was the year when inflation really took off), including new fire regulations, an outbreak (serious) of dry rot, Dutch Elm disease which laid low most of the beautiful trees which surrounded the property, and a variety of other contretemps, large and small. And, having survived all this, it must surely give heart to other similar ventures, even if, literally speaking, it does not do so to the Department of Education and Science.

In 1973, I was hardly in a position to be of any help. As I had not attended any meetings, I had heard of the project and no more – if I remember correctly, from Mrs Elgar herself. To me, as I was situated then, the idea shone out like a mirage in the desert. For whatever happened to the rest of the family, if this dream became a reality, it would at least offer a haven to Simon. By then, it had already been decided that Mrs Elgar was to run the school, and, very tentatively, not giving all my reasons, I asked her if she would consider taking Simon in the first group of pupils. She was very willing. As at Ealing, she needed a careful balance of more and less severely disturbed children. Later, after my husband had actually left us, I confirmed my request, and made the necessary application to the county education authorities, since the fees were way beyond my resources.

I know now that I did not at the time fully appreciate the momentous import of that decision. I was in a state of great shock and considerable panic, terrified of breaking down, terrified of dying. Simon lay near the source of this panic, for of all my children he was undoubtedly the most completely vulnerable, without the slightest means of defending himself in any way. I could not bear to think what would happen to him if I, too, failed him. It did not seem likely that my husband's mistress could entertain much compassion for him, let alone patience, or love. There was no one else.

Thus the Somerset Court project offered me peace of mind at least in one area of my life. If Simon went there, he would not be going to strangers, but to teachers he already knew and trusted, to share his days with schoolfellows to whose idiosyncracies he was already accustomed. Above all, if he went there, he would have no more disruptions of his now shattered world. He would have a chance to learn to do something, to look after animals and plants, make things, to be, in short, a person with a useful place in society, a certain dignity. It seemed to be all I wanted for him, and what I, in my depressed and apathetic state, could not even start to give him. All I had to offer in those days was tears, and remorse, and love. It certainly did not seem enough.

Friends and advisers were unanimous in supporting me in my decision, and in emphasizing my near-miraculous good fortune that I was in a position to make it at all. I was not unaware of this. It could hardly escape my attention that, out of all the thousands of autistic children in the country, Simon was to be one of the handful who would receive exactly the kind of education he needed, for as long as he needed it. The decision to send him away could not possibly, it seemed to me, be a wrong one. I had to look ahead, as clinically as possible, and do what was best for him. I also had to try to do what seemed best for my other children, who might otherwise face a burden in the future which could well threaten their own happiness.

It was, therefore, with very few doubts that, nine months after the break-up of our family, I drove Simon to Ealing where, in front of a battery of TV cameras all set to give the school the publicity it needed, he boarded the coach that was to take him and his fellows down the motorways to Somerset. And as we watched the coach drive off, and waved, and smiled, and registered happiness and relief for the benefit of the cameras, I remember suddenly being aware of a chill inside me. I had just sent someone else away. It was the first touch of emotional reality in the whole affair. And when I returned home, there was another empty place at table, another empty bed, another gap in my daily life. Slowly, I began to realize what I had, in fact, done. But even then, I could not anticipate the development of those feelings, the present enormity of my sense of loss.

No doubt our exceptional circumstances make this feeling worse than it is likely to be for ordinary, whole families, in that they cut us off physically from Somerset Court. Not only are we a one-parent family with the three normal children in my sole care, living on a tight budget, but two of the three normal children are exceptionally gifted, which means that they make extra demands. I have to try to be very clinical about the amount of physical and mental strain I can take, since extra strain on me inevitably has repercussions on the children. The solo drive to and from Somerset Court in one day, in order to take Simon out for a meal, which is what the other parents do several times a term on "Visiting Sundays", is, except on very rare occasions, beyond my resources, both financial and physical. I can hardly feel happy about this.

Also, although Simon comes home for school holidays, travelling by coach to the central meeting point at Ealing, only at Christmas and Easter do his holidays coincide with those of the other children, all on a three-term year. In practical terms this means for me that, between mid-June and mid-October, there is always someone on holiday from school. For many parents, having their handicapped child around when the others are at school is a blessing, in that the handicapped one makes excessive demands, but this is not the case for us. For me, it is far, far easier to entertain Simon when the others are at home, and he can be treated as an ordinary member of the family, and when the highly taxing schedule of music lessons and school functions is temporarily in abeyance. All of which makes me feel that I am not, as it were, in gear with Somerset Court. The one weekend a year which I take off, and spend in Somerset so that I may visit Simon, somehow makes me feel worse, not better, and more than ever a piece of social flotsam.

Physically, therefore, we are unavoidably cut off from Simon, unless we weigh anchors and go to live in Somerset, which, again, is hardly fair on the other children. This feeling is bad enough in itself, but largely because his handicap is what it is, I find I am becoming increasingly cut off from him emotionally. Because he now lives far from me, and cannot speak or write to me spontaneously, Simon himself can do nothing to help preserve the once strong bonds between us. He speaks far less than he once did, though he understands far more. All my questions are answered by the "yes" that he thinks is expected of him. This means that what time I do have alone with him I find hard to use to our mutual profit – I have lost the skill of making contact. As I can only guess at the texture of his daily life, at his thoughts and feelings, I cannot share his problems, just as he cannot share mine. I cannot help him.

Four times a year, we parents and other interested people receive a newsletter, composed of contributions from Mrs Elgar, visitors to the school, parents, and from time to time – this is a supreme joy – from the most articulate ·children themselves. I seize on my newsletters, for they are a contact of a kind, and contain accounts of school outings and functions, visitors' impressions, etc. But, avidly though I read them, I find the experience rather akin to reading someone else's biography. Nothing that happens involves me. It is all so far away. For me, being involved in a school means taking part in at least some of its daily life, being able to visit it, to get to know the teachers, attend the functions, help even if only to a small degree, to experience the feel of the place. School, after all, occupies a large share of my children's time, plays a vital part in their development, and as a parent I need to feel that I have some personal connection with it.

Geographical distance from a school makes this connection extremely difficult to maintain, even when the children concerned are normal. When they are handicapped, I am not sure that I can see how it can possibly be done, unless the parents involved have no other responsibilities, and are wealthy enough to make light of the cost of travel.

This is a factor which I now feel very strongly should be carefully taken into account when a family is considering placing a handicapped child in a school or community a long way from home. Be the institution ever so loving, be it ever so caring, it cannot possibly maintain the child's ties with the family at their former strength. And if the relationships within that family had been strong ones before the placement, then the loss of the child will be felt not only by the parents, but by the brothers and sisters, to a point where some emotional damage can take place, and feelings of guilt and bitterness be engendered.

This has happened to us to a degree which, when I made the decision to send him away, I could not possibly have foreseen. When one is suffering from depression, one cannot imagine what it is like to feel happy again. I could not know, in 1974, that we would in fact one day be happy again, and move around actively despite, as it were, the loss of a leg. We can do this because we have become a highly coordinated unit, with each child aware of his or her special importance as a contributor, and taking a pride in the success of the whole. This lessens jealousies, and helps bring about a far greater degree of tolerance despite great differences in personalities. But Simon is our weak spot. Each time he leaves us again to return to school, he leaves behind him tears and sad faces. The others miss him acutely. Joy reigns the day he is due to come home on holiday, and his place is once more set at table.

This is an unhappiness that shows as yet no sign of healing. It is not one I can dispel with rational arguments, and promises that his living at boarding school is for his own good. There is no answer to the words, "I miss him terribly, Mummy".

Had I been less in a state of shock at the time of making the decision, I might perhaps have thought this out for myself. Especially as one social worker did actually say that it was best for me to accustom myself to the severance of the maternal bond, to hearing my son refer to his school as "home", to seeing him less and less, and that all this was best both for him and for me. I could not digest the implications of the words at the time, but they remained in my memory. I realize now what they mean. My reaction is one of outrage, outrage every bit as violent as it would have been if, like some parents I know, I had been told to put my newly diagnosed baby away in a home and forget it. Those who can give such advice in cold blood, although it may present all the appearances of common sense, cannot possibly have any fundamental knowledge of human nature.

As a caring parent, I thus find myself pinned between two opposing forces, *which should not be opposing*: the one which decrees what is best for Simon, both socially and emotionally, and the one which decides what is best for the rest of the family. It seems to me that our modern Welfare State, for all its liberal attitudes, is, when it comes to basics, as Victorian as any of our asylum building fore-fathers. It is more convenient, and more economical, to isolate the mentally handicapped. As I see it, from a parent's point of view, Simon and his like need both the emotional experience of loving family life as well as support and training as members of the larger community. Clearly, the difficulties of achieving this are multifarious, but in my experience, once aims become clear, difficulties have a way of diminishing.

Much is spoken these days about the rights of children. But I think that parents, too, have *some* rights. In order to gain for my son the education and training he requires in order to play any useful part in society, I have had to give up my rights as a mother. Of course I have the right to withdraw him from Somerset Court tomorrow – only then I would find myself in the teeth of the opposing wind, for nowhere else would he receive such training as he receives there. I cannot, it seems, have it both ways.

Of course, had Simon been normal, and I been rich, I might have chosen to send him away to boarding school. But I would have had a choice between two viable alternatives. Again, had Simon been normal, he would have eventually left home as a matter of course to pursue his career, and to set up some kind of household of his own. But since communication would always have been possible, barring a breakdown in the relationship, a strong link of friendship and affection would have survived the stresses of maturation to enrich us both.

But Simon is not normal, and never will be, and I am aware that the links I worked so hard to form are flaking away, one by one. This is part of my bitterness at being left alone with the problem. For, had our marriage continued, the pressures would have been less great. Far more physical access would have been possible, for the rigours of driving could have been shared, and the expenses of food and petrol less sharply felt. That, however, like so much else, is of course a matter of the "might have been" relegated to the realm of pure speculation.

The present is here, and actual, and the bitterness with it. I cannot see how it can positively be modified.

So here I am, back once more on my now-familiar two levels. My reason, knowing of the struggles, the anxieties, the despair of others in their search for adequate education for their autistic children, insists that we are fantastically lucky, that I am discontented with a seat in Paradise. Simon is safe, cared for with love and expertise. The atmosphere at Somerset Court, on the few occasions when I have experienced it, is one of happy, purposeful activity, where Simon occupies his own, individual place. After depositing him there, on return from the family holiday, I have driven away with the other three children, rejoicing in our luck. Yet, as the miles accumulated behind us, the forced note in the rejoicing became plain, and the silences stretched further and further, as the absence in the front seat beside me became more and more palpable. How could we be lucky, when we had left him behind?

And, indeed, in the eyes of everyone else, he *is* lucky. He *is* safe, safe from my death or his father's, safe from murderous cars, rapacious men, or disorientated thugs. He is leading a useful life with his plants and his animals. He need not feel a total parasite, if he were capable of formulating such a concept, for he costs the ratepayer less than he would if he were in a mental sub-normality hospital – in fact, eventually, if Somerset Court prospers, he may well cost the ratepayer nothing at all.

So, on this level, I can and must accept his life at Somerset Court, and am thankful for it, and grateful to all those who help him achieve it. I am grateful too for the lessening of my own physical burden at this time when I need every part of my strength.

But inside me, I cannot silence that other voice, the voice that quietly, continuously mourns his loss. I do not just mean his loss to me. I mean also his own loss in terms of his own identity, his personality which is moulded by his membership of an ordinary human family. A little of it still remains, as when he immediately asks "Where's Joanna?" when he arrives home, with a flash of his old smile. But nowadays he no longer looks us in the eye as he once did – at least, not until he has been at home for several days. He looks persistently away, leaving me to guess uneasily at his feelings. Then, after a while, he seems to relax with us all again, to become once more his old self, the self which went cheerfully off to the ESN school every day, when he still had a father around, and a mother who was not constantly and incomprehensibly lapsing into tears. But as the return to school approaches, his eyes and thoughts avoid us once again, as if he wants nothing more to do with us.

Only once have I known his deeper feelings to become unmistakable. One evening a couple of months ago, their father phoned the children from abroad, and spoke to Simon along with the others. We had been watching television. When he returned to sit with us, I became aware after a few minutes that he was weeping silently, the tears streaming down his cheeks, his eyes fixed unseeingly on the wall. He wept all evening, and would not be comforted – even pushing us away quite violently, for him. I have never felt so helpless, and so full of pity and anger in my life.

Yet perhaps those tears were not altogether a bad thing. They proved to me that he is still one of us, that he has not lost everything that marked him as one of us. I needed the proof.

Simon needs specialized help, that is undeniable. Yet, equally, he needs love, love that is uniquely for him, as an individual, the kind of love for which there is no substitute. Because our society is as it is, because we cannot, it seems, as the poet Langland recommends, have him into our houses and help him when he comes, because of the deep flaws in our own natures, he cannot have both.

To which I would say that the loss is society's, as well as his.

11

Time Present

Those who have Whitgift blood, says old Tom Shoesmith, alias Puck, in Rudyard Kipling's *Puck of Pook's Hill*, "No Trouble 'ud lie on, no Maid 'ud sigh on, no Night could frighten, no Harm could make sin, an' no Woman could make a fool of."

When I look at Simon now, fifteen years old, and six feet tall, it occurs to me that this is a very fair general description of him, as well as of the Bee Boy, the one of Whitgift stock. As I look, it is very hard to connect this strange young man with that perfect baby, featured so often in my snapshot album, of whom I was so proud all those years ago.

The marvellous beauty of childhood has fallen away now. Adolescence sits no more gracefully on Simon than it does on other boys of his age. This is sad in a way, but it no longer matters as it once did. For years that beauty was of great value to me, acting as a solace, helping me to recover from the shock of the diagnosis. If in some ways it was a rather cruel solace, in that it intensified my frustration at not being able to awaken the intelligence it seemed to express, at least it helped me to come to terms gradually with the reality of Simon.

This reality is far clearer nowadays. Now that he is of adult size and proportions, the unfocused appearance of his eyes, the general lack of expressiveness in the features, and of purposefulness in his gait reveal his disabilities far more quickly than they did when he was a child. This is surely in part because one expects more of the face of an adult, so that childish immaturity of feature, and childish love of grimaces come as something of a shock.

Physically, Simon is almost fully developed, a phenomenon

which seems to have taken him by surprise, as if the bodily spurt to maturity had happened without his knowledge or consent. This is, of course, the case with most normal boys – but they have the advantage which Simon does not have of being able to ask about the changes that worry them, and being able at least to some extent to understand the answers. Simon asks no questions. He shows, in fact, very little concern over the majority of the developments that have taken place in his body. He appears puzzled, at times, by the sheer length of his arms and legs, and you can see him wondering where to put them, but, with a couple of exceptions, he shows little interest in this new, large self that has grown upon him.

His physical maturity is, however, a cause of somewhat greater concern to those who care for him, since it raises problems concerning his integration with normal people which had not existed when he was a child among children.

Being of dark complexion, much of his facial hair has been visible for some time, to the point where regular shaving has now become necessary. Although the hair is still mainly down, its presence seemed to emphasize his handicap, making his skin look muddy and uncared for. I realized that an electric razor would be the easiest answer for all concerned, and we were lucky enough to be given one for him. This has been a great success, he loves both the sound and the sensation on his skin. "Moustache all gone!" he shouts when the job is complete. This is fine as far as it goes, but I am finding it hard to make him understand why the job needs doing at all, and when precisely it is necessary to do it.

Dress raises similar problems of understanding. He cannot comprehend the conventions and the motivations which lie behind our choice of clothes. As it is important for him that he should appear as acceptable as possible to the majority of people, careful training is necessary if he is not, quite unwittingly, to give offence. He is such a creature of habit and ritual that it has not been too difficult to teach him to keep those parts of his body covered which the general public considers it undesirable to see, but I have to beware situations which are unusual for him, such as changing on the beach. This did not matter at all when he was younger, but it matters a great deal now, and he has had to learn this if he is not to cause great embarrassment to his sister and brothers and their friends. They can choose to swim in the nude if they wish, but as Simon works by habit rather than by conscious choice, it would be extremely unwise to set him such an example. I also try to teach him that there are good clothes and working clothes – not because I hold any very strong views on this myself, but because other, especially older people, do, and he cannot afford to offend them by turning up to functions in gloriously incongruous garb. Other teenagers can get away with sartorial revolt, but Simon does not have this freedom. He needs to please, to be trained in habits of cleanliness, neatness, and grooming – to give him at least a certain dignity in the eyes of strangers. Again, his ritualistic tendencies can be put to use, so that his structured day contains definite times for personal hygiene, and nothing gets overlooked. He is perfectly able to dress by himself, to manage buttons and bows, but he cannot really select clothes, and is quite thrown when the customary circumstances change, and we go on holiday, for instance.

One of the aspects of autistic adolescence for which I was stupidly ill-prepared, perhaps out of sub-conscious fear, was what to expect from him by way of sexual behaviour. Fortunately, those of my friends with pubescent daughters were sensible enough to voice their own concern lest Simon's obsessive tendencies should take a turn in the direction of the girls, with what could have been disastrous results both for them and for him. I suddenly realized all the implications, and flew for help to the psychiatrist friend who had advised me before. From him I received what was in one sense complete reassurance, in another what seemed like the closing of the last chink in the invisible barrier shutting off my son from the rest of us. Autistic people, he told me, simply could not experience sufficient emotional drive to make the sexual act possible for them. They could not enter into a relationship close or deep enough to rouse the necessary feeling. They are condemned by their handicap to lifelong solitude, denied this the most primitive of comforts, enjoyed even by animals.

I wondered if any autistic people, those with the highest degree of mental ability and verbal ability, could understand their own deprivation, and difference. I hoped not, for their sakes. In Simon's case I do not think that he is actually aware of the differences between him and other people, but still I cannot

be sure. Often he surprises me, and I realize that he understands far more than I think.

In terms of purely practical care, the words were, however,
extremely reassuring. They eliminated a host of threatening
difficulties. I could repeat them, for the psychiatrist was an
authority on the subject, to all my friends, who consequently
ceased to worry about Simon's presence in their homes. It has
become increasingly obvious, in any case, that he is not in the
least interested in the physical charms of the various teenage
girls we know, and he is one viewer who remains consistently
unmoved by the daily displays on television. The only girl
whom, to my knowledge, he ever touches, is Joanna, and his
interest in her does not appear to have developed beyond its
childhood form of stroking and smelling her newly washed
hair, and games of tickling and romping which have nothing
exploratory about them, but which I don't encourage, just in
case.

The only two changes which do provoke his continuous interest are his ever-increasing height, and his breaking voice. He
now towers above the rest of us, which seems to delight him. He
adores the cries of admiration which greet him when he returns
home, and submits happily to the ceremony of being dragged
off for measurement to the kitchen door-frame. "Simon *big* boy
now," he chuckles as the tape reveals yet another increase,
and I look despairingly at the gap between his sock and his
trouser leg. As he now threatens to exceed the height of the
door frames in our very old house he will soon discover the
penalties of this increase in stature, somewhat painfully, and I
have visions of him walking round with a permanently bowed
head.

The voice change is distinctly comic, and gives him and us,
if not always other people, considerable amusement. He is so
naïvely intrigued by this odd phenomenon, so delighted with
the variety of experimental sounds that he can make with this
suddenly unreliable instrument, that he often has us all in fits
of laughter. He has, as I have already described, always liked
singing, but of course he is accustomed to singing the treble
line. Habits die hard with autistic people, and the weird falsetto
that startles the rest of the congregation at church is Simon's
attempt at a compromise. Now and again he succeeds in
pitching his new, deep voice accurately, and clearly revels in the

result, but invariably he loses his line again, and a puzzled expression steals over his face. He also revels in the family plaudits of his "deep, deep voice", and deepens it yet further for our admiration. No doubt he will eventually find his niche again on the bass line, but the process cannot be hurried.

He has recently added one more to his list of accomplishments. Last year, at Somerset Court, he finally consented to take his hand off the polystyrene float, which was little but a psychological aid to his general buoyancy, and swim. This in fact represents a major victory, which has taken years of patient effort to bring about, for I remember his early nervousness in the water very vividly, nervousness which gradually lost ground to his instinctive love of the element. For years he had been content merely to stand, taste and feel it. It was truly wonderful to see him enjoy the sensation of floating in it. A swimming teacher friend of mine, who has done her share of patient advice and instruction with Simon, promptly awarded him the Swimming Teachers' Association "Endeavour" badge. There were tears in both our eyes as we watched him grunt his way across the pool. His huge pleasure is obvious, though in the public pool he attracts reproachful looks from other bathers as his long, fiercely kicking legs send tidal waves over their heads. I prefer to take him swimming in the sea, where his indifference to the discomfort of others is less of a nuisance, but we live inland, so that I only relax fully in his enjoyment when we go on holiday. Many people in our local pool know us, and make allowances, but there are always those who don't. It is good, whatever the frowns, to see him getting much of the exercise he needs this way, with such obvious enjoyment, since otherwise his general tendency to passive indolence could easily lead to a flabby, overweight body.

Fortunately, in this respect, he also enjoys long walks. Not that he tells us so in so many words, but he always responds quickly when the cry "Boots on" rings round the house. A walk with Simon, however, is not a very companionable affair. He seems positively to dislike walking beside anyone. Unless I insist that he stay by me, he is always to be found striding out on his long legs a good distance in front of me, or lingering dreamily far behind. Usually it seems kinder to let him go his own pace, but just occasionally, if we are going shopping together, or attending some social function, I do insist that he walk beside me, giving me his arm. He acquiesces, usually with a little smile that seems to say, "Alright, I'll humour her this once", but proceeds to fold the required arm as stiff as a ramrod, only, the moment my attention strays, to let it fall gently back into its habitual position, while his steps gradually desert the rhythm of mine. He bears a very striking resemblance to his father, and, now that he is the same size, it is hard not to wince at this touching of still recent scars: *this* rejection is not, after all, a deliberate one. I can think of few gestures that would give me keener pleasure than to have my arm spontaneously taken by Simon, and to have him give it the occasional affectionate squeeze, as his brothers and sister do. It seems such a small thing to ask, and such a huge thing to be denied.

It is hard for the other children too, in that Simon's size and his physical appearance make him something of a father figure to them. I can never fill the place of that missing father. Instinctively, they turn to the big, solid, male figure of their elder brother, only to find that he, no more than I, can supply them with the paternal affection they need so sorely.

Still, although we are denied these gestures of affection which would mean so much to us, we are comforted in that it is possible to see that Simon does experience the emotion itself. We can see it in his smile, though this is less frequent than in former days, and in the way he is constantly touching us, as if to reassure himself that we are still there. When he is at home, he constantly repeats my name, "Mummy", and it is incumbent on me always to reply, otherwise he comes anxiously in search of me. This, small as it is, is better than nothing, and I know full well that many parents of autistic children get absolutely nothing. His smile of affection is not reserved for family and teachers alone – certain of my friends are very special to him. Perhaps the chief of these is my next door neighbour. She and I are very close friends, and I think Simon is aware of this. He responds exceptionally to her feeling for him. She has become one of the constants of his life at home, and he never spends any time with us without going in to visit her. A lunch out together in a small local restaurant is not half the treat unless she comes too, and admires his prodigious appetite. In fact, wherever he receives a constant, and it has to be constant, show of attention and warm affection he responds, and this is very moving to see. Unlike his alarms and excursions of early days, he now enjoys going out visiting, and relaxes in my friends' houses as easily as he would in his own, provided that they are well stocked with jigsaw puzzles, which is his favourite leisure occupation, and that they are good and generous cooks! He is not even upset by staying away from home overnight, and the screams and howls of early days now seem like a bad dream.

He has retained his extraordinary memory. It serves him in ways that sometimes startle the rest of us. His sense of direction, for instance, is quite phenomenal. My friend next door was amazed to see how, on our second visit to a certain small restaurant, which occurred after a gap of several months, he loped ahead of us, turned in the door, and seated himself expectantly at the very table where we had sat on our previous visit. She was greatly tickled. An even better example is the occasion, just before my husband's departure, when we took Simon and Joanna to the opera. As usual, my husband had taken a box, but this turned out to be very difficult of access – one had to thread one's way through a large and very crowded dress circle, out and through a network of little corridors, before eventually stumbling upon a choice of doors. During the interval my husband deemed it prudent to take Simon to visit the loo, which turned out to be far away beyond the other side of the dress circle. I took no particular notice when Simon arrived back alone, and calmly resumed his seat, assuming that my husband had stopped to buy ice creams or talk to a friend en route. It was in fact a good time before he, too, arrived, looking somewhat green, and, not at once noticing Simon who was in a corner of the box, announced that he had lost him in the loo! He was both relieved and amazed when he eventually saw that Simon had already returned. He had accomplished the tortuous journey back, in a strange place, completely alone, and without apparently turning a hair. It was a feat that would have floored many an adult. If only he could communicate, I feel sure that Simon would have a brilliant career as a navigator!

Reading over all my attempts at description of Simon, I feel that they are hopelessly fragmented. Upon reflection, however, I realize that they can hardly be anything else since they are composed almost totally of my observations and impressions. Simon himself cannot contribute the unifying element of his own words and thoughts. I have to guess at them, and it is fatally easy to make the mistake of reading too much into the clues. The unity of the portrait is therefore a projection of my own mind, unsupported by Simon, and is thus in a way suspect. This must be born in mind. Simon cannot correct my false impressions.

All the same, false though they might prove if he could speak and tell me different, they are true in as much as they are all mine, and that I have lived with Simon for a long time, loving him and trying always to help him. If my description resembles a pointilliste painting, it is because no other style would serve as well. It was comparatively easy to show him as a baby, with a baby's simpler patterns of behaviour. It was already less easy when he was a child, chiefly because of our isolation, which precluded helpful comparisons and deprived me of the least clue as to what future development might entail. My attitudes then tended to be coloured by an optimism which subsequently proved false: although he has undoubtedly improved, Simon is not articulate, and I think now that he probably never will be. The adolescent is an even more difficult subject, for I know even less about the possibilities of his development over the next ten years, and I have, in any case, this frightening feeling that I am losing contact with him.

Let me at least try to draw the picture together. I see a tall boy with the verbal comprehension of a six year old, though with far less spontaneous speech, on the edge of physical manhood. He is totally unaware of, and unworried by what the future does or does not hold for him. His two small worlds of home and Somerset Court make sense for him, because on the whole they move in ordered patterns, peopled by the same set of characters. His contentment depends on a constant supply of affection and praise, and good food. He is bitterly distressed by anger or criticism, which obviously to him imply the withdrawal of love. Outside these two small worlds he is lost, utterly dependent on the good-will of puzzled strangers to supply his needs and give him direction. Most of these will rarely, if ever, have encountered his handicap, and may well be alarmed by it, unaware of his gentleness.

For he is, just as when he was a child, totally without aggression – which is just as well, since a blow from him would make mincemeat of me. Despite his size, he has remained one of the gentlest people I know. He is still, also, at least at home, one of the most docile. His flare for self-assertion died away when Marianne left, never to return. It may seem odd, but there are days when I long for him to resist me, to make some show of independence, to declare himself as a separate human being, as Joanna is beginning to do, as any other adolescent would. But he never does.

He cannot share his feelings with us, even though we are sure they exist. He can no more tell us of his misery and anger at the loss of his father than he can of his sunnier experiences. If we try to interpret his feelings from his expression or his tears, and try to comfort him, he will have none of it. He will not have us near him. He is alone in everything. Only when he is physically ill, which is not often, will he accept loving care. But even when he suffered a couple of small fits (many autistic adolescents are prone to these) during his first year at Somerset Court, which frightened him greatly, he could not accept our reassurances.

Despite this intense emotional solitude, it is obvious that he likes to be part of a group, with a role to play in it, even if he cannot sustain that role for very long. He smiles with pleasure when I ask him to perform household tasks along with the other children, and performs them far more neatly and efficiently than I would myself (thanks to Mrs Elgar!) The feeling of inclusion matters as much as ever it did, even when he has no comprehension whatsoever of the object of the expedition.

Sometimes, when he is at home, I catch myself looking at him with a certain wonder. There was no way I could have foreseen this young man of the present. No ancestors could point his way, his handicap eradicated the traits of heredity. The growth of my friends' children could offer me no guide, nor even that of other autistic children, since they differ from one another individually just as much as normal children. Nor is it any easier to foresee the grown man of the future, to imagine his adult identity. His well-being, his development, hang on threads still more slender than do those of the rest of us. For at least to some extent we shape our future by the choices we make each day of our lives.

For Simon there can be no choices. He has no say in the ordering of his days.

This is the outstanding fact which, as I look both ways, backwards and forwards, forms the unity of the picture. As a child, as an adolescent, and as an adult, he has been, and will be denied free will. He is totally dependent on the will of others. He is completely innocent. And he is vulnerable. The whole texture of his life is created by the rest of us, by our thoughtlessness, our neglect, our cruelties, our incompetence, and by our care and our love.

I do not think the poet Langland pointed out Simon's importance to us lightly.

Conclusion

"To make an end is to make a beginning"

The ambivalence in the sub-title of this book is deliberate. If it is not clear whether I am referring to the experience of my autistic child himself, or whether it is to my, or come to that, to the other children's experience of what it is like to live with him, it is because all these sets of experience are inextricably intertwined. His handicap affected our lives profoundly. The way we reacted to the discovery of it, both consciously and unconsciously, affected his reaction. We are interdependent.

It is over a decade now since the first part of my life ended, and I set out along the long, hard road predicted by the paediatrician. It has indeed been hard, and I hope that I have not given a different impression. But what he did not predict, perhaps because he did not know me very well, and perhaps because in any case it was unpredictable, was the friendship, the charity, the love and the joy I would also find along the way, giving me the strength to survive even in the worst stretches. John Bunyan would have recognized them all, but at the time of the diagnosis I had not read my Bunyan since childhood.

It was the joy which amazed me the most. Earlier in my life I would not have believed it possible. This was real joy – not to be mistaken for the elation of the drug addict, or the fanaticism of the extremist, both of which tend to leave the personality diminished. This was a fundamental joy to be found in a new awareness of living, pared down to its essential elements, needing very little material sustenance in order to thrive. It came into being as I watched Simon's pleasure in textures – smoothness, furriness, silkiness; in tastes – the saltiness of the sea, the acidity of citrous fruit, the composite taste of human skin; in smells – the smell of hair and skin, the smell of milk, the smell of new clothes. It flowered as I saw him beaming with the wind in his hair, clinging to the back of a cantering pony. It multiplied as I watched the glow of achievement in his eyes when he finally succeeded in riding his bicycle, and later in swimming across the swimming pool.

This joy that was Simon's gift to me gave me what was perhaps my only chance of growing, emotionally and spiritually. He gave it to Joanna, Tom and David, too. For, tasting it, all of us, however young, were compelled to pause before rushing out to compete with the world, to join in the hustling, jostling crowd of Vanity Fair. Here, given us freely, was our chance to realize that there was no need.

Later, when our lives passed into what seemed then like a black, endless tunnel, and all joy, great or small, seemed impossible, the memory of it, the habit of it, as it were, gave us strength to go on, to survive, and eventually to emerge at the other end not weaker, but stronger, with our eyes opened to infinitely wider horizons.

Our discovery of joy shaped Simon's life. He has grown up in an atmosphere of acceptance and love. He has grown up trusting people, even though he cannot understand them. This is not true of many who are autistic. I worried lest he should feel betrayed when he left home to live at Somerset Court, so soon after his father leaving us. I still do. But at least I am certain of one essential point: that Mrs Elgar's love is there to carry on where mine, in his eyes at least, falls short. With one exception, he has never known anything but continuous affection.

This, were he to live and work out in the wild world, would be a disadvantage terrifying to think of. The world is not an affectionate place. Evil is present, in many forms, everywhere. And he would not stand the slightest chance, were he to meet it.

The sheltered community where he lives is not a normal community in that, to everyone's knowledge, it is free from evil. It exists to protect Simon and his like, to enable them to live useful and dignified lives despite their vulnerability. It is not the perfect answer, for the price to be paid for such protection is heavy, as I have shown, but no one has as yet come up with a better. I would prefer Simon to grow up far from us in such a shelter, than as a drugged automaton, or as a despised outcast.

Perhaps we shall never find the perfect answer. After all, no society has ever yet discovered how to achieve complete protection of the weak and the helpless.

Realizing this, perhaps I shall find the strength to carry me through the painful, but, it seems, inevitable change of relationship with him that lies ahead – but of that I cannot be sure. Once I am convinced that living away from home is the best and only answer for him, the strength will surely come – even though the road grows no easier.

I think that something of this feeling was in the hearts of all us parents as we sat watching and listening to the children's concert last year at Somerset Court, and that this was what filled our eyes with tears as we listened to Dilys singing. Dilys would not look at us, the audience. Her eyes turned continuously, in small, furtive, quick glances, like a shy animal's to Mrs Elgar, as she sat at the side of the stage. Her voice was a small, pure, true soprano, utterly poignant. And she sang to us the ancient words of the twenty-third Psalm, set to the tune of Crimond. They might not have been the experience of everyone there, but at least they had, so far, been hers, as they have, on the whole so far, been Simon's:

> "Goodness and mercy all my days
> Shall surely follow me:
> And in God's house forever more
> My dwelling-place shall be."

Appendix

THE HANDICAPS OF AUTISTIC CHILDREN
by Dr Lorna Wing, LMD, DPM
(from *Communication*, the NSAC publication, June 1972)

A BASIC IMPAIRMENTS

1 Language problems

(a) Spoken language
    (i) Severe problems in comprehension of speech
   (ii) Abnormalities in the use of speech (in those children who do not remain mute):
      Immediate echolalia
      Delayed echolalia
      Repetitive, stereotyped, inflexible use of words and phrases
      Confusion over the use of pronouns
      Immaturity of grammatical structure of spontaneous (not echoed) speech
      Aphasia in spontaneous (not echoed) speech (i.e. muddling of sequence of letters and words, confusion of words of similar sound or related meaning, problems with prepositions, conjunctions and other small linking words, etc.)
  (iii) Poor control of pitch, volume and intonation of voice
  (iv) Problems of pronunciation

(b) "Non-spoken" language
    (i) Poor comprehension of the information conveyed by gesture, miming, facial expression, bodily posture, etc.
    (ii) Lack of use of gesture, miming, facial expression and bodily posture, etc., to convey information (the only "gesture" may be grabbing someone else's hand and pulling them towards a desired object)

2 Perceptual problems

    (i) Unusual response to sounds (indifference, distress, fascination)
    (ii) Unusual response to visual stimuli (indifference, distress, fascination)
    (iii) Unusual response to pain and cold (indifference, over reaction)
    (iv) Unusual response to being touched (pushing away when touched lightly but enjoying tickling and romping)
    (v) "Paradoxical" responses to sensations (e.g. covering eyes in response to a sound, or ears in response to a visual stimulus)
    (vi) A tendency to use peripheral rather than central visual fields (responding to movement and outline rather than to details; looking past rather than at people and things)
    (vii) A tendency to inspect people and things with brief rapid glances rather than a steady gaze

3 Problems of motor control and directional orientation

    (i) Jumping, flapping limbs and grimacing when excited
    (ii) Difficulty in *copying* skilled movements made by others (unless child is taught by having his own limbs moved)
    (iii) *Spontaneous* large movements, or fine skilled movements, may be clumsy in some children, although others appear to be graceful and nimble

(iv) Tendency to muddle right-left, up and down, back and front

(v) A springy tip-toe walk, without appropriate swinging of the arms

4 Various abnormalities of physical development, autonomic function and vestibular control

including:

(i) Immaturity of bone growth

(ii) Abnormalities of heart rate and temperature control

(iii) Erratic patterns of sleeping and resistance to the effects of sedatives and hypnotics

(iv) Lack of dizziness after spinning round, and other abnormalities of vestibular control

B SPECIAL SKILLS (contrasting with lack of skill in other areas)

1 Skills which do not involve language, e.g. music, arithmetic, dismantling and assembling mechanical or electrical objects, fitting together jig saws or constructional toys.

2 An unusual form of memory which seems to allow the prolonged storage of items in the exact form in which they were first perceived, e.g. phrases or whole conversations spoken by other people, poems, long lists e.g. of all the Kings of England, long passages of music, the route to a certain place, the arrangement of a collection of pebbles, the steps to be followed in a routine activity, a complicated visual pattern, etc. The items selected for storage do not appear, on any criteria used by normal people, to be of any special importance, and they are stored without being "interpreted" or changed.

C SECONDARY BEHAVIOUR PROBLEMS

1 Apparent aloofness and indifference to other people (although enjoying some forms of active physical contact).

2 Intense resistance to change and attachment to objects and routines.

3 Inability to play imaginatively with objects, toys or other children or adults; or to imitate other people's actions in an imaginative, creative way.

4 Lack of understanding of the purpose of any pursuits which do not bring on immediate and obvious sensory reward and which involve an understanding of language and symbols (i.e. school work, games, hobbies, social conversation, literature, poetry, etc.) and a consequent lack of motivation to indulge in these activities, even if the necessary skills are available to the child.

5 A tendency to select for attention minor or trivial aspects of things in the environment instead of taking in the meaning of the whole scene (e.g. attending to one ear ring instead of a whole person, a wheel instead of the whole toy train, a switch instead of the whole piece of electrical apparatus, etc.).

6 Lack of fear of real danger, excessive fear of some harmless objects or situations and other inappropriate emotional reactions.

7 A search for simple, understandable sensations through touch, taste, smell, stereotyped movements, manipulation of objects and, sometimes, through self-injury.

8 Socially immature and difficult behaviour.

9 A tendency to appear odd and "mechanical" in voice, facial expression, posture and movement.